Samuel G. Green

The Kingdoms Of Israel And Judah

Part 1. To the Fall of the israelite Monarchy

Samuel G. Green

The Kingdoms Of Israel And Judah
Part 1. To the Fall of the israelite Monarchy

ISBN/EAN: 9783337315825

Printed in Europe, USA, Canada, Australia, Japan

Cover: Foto ©Lupo / pixelio.de

More available books at **www.hansebooks.com**

THE
KINGDOMS OF ISRAEL AND JUDAH

AFTER THE DISRUPTION.

By SAMUEL G. GREEN, D.D.,

LATE PRESIDENT OF RAWDON COLLEGE, LEEDS; AUTHOR OF "THE APOSTLE PETER, HIS LIFE AND LETTERS," ETC.

PART I.

TO THE FALL OF THE ISRAELITE MONARCHY.

LONDON:
SUNDAY SCHOOL UNION,
56, OLD BAILEY, E.C.

PREFACE.

THE following sketch has been prepared for the use of Sunday School Teachers. It has not, therefore, been thought necessary to enter upon questions of minute or abstruse criticism, which, however interesting, have but little relation to the practical utility of the history.

To prevent misconception, it may here be distinctly stated, as will indeed be apparent throughout the volume, that the narratives in Kings and Chronicles respectively are adopted as of equal authority. What author or authors compiled the former, and who was the "chronicler" that supplemented the earlier record, it may be impossible for us to ascertain; the books alike are given to us "by inspiration of God." At the same time their respective purposes are different; a due consideration of this fact may explain some apparent inconsistencies; and it is hoped that in the following pages few, if any, real difficulties arising from the comparison of the two books have been passed over.

The Notes appended to each chapter refer to matters of interest which could not well have been considered in the course of what aimed to be a succinct and continuous narrative. It is hoped that the marginal references will also be found serviceable to the student; the texts there quoted being for the most part passages which lie away from the main course of the sacred history. The citation of chapter and verse for every particular in the narrative would have been unnecessary for readers familiar with the Bible.

CONTENTS.

CHAPTER I.
THE DISRUPTION 1

CHAPTER II.
THE TWO KINGDOMS, TO THE FALL OF JEROBOAM'S HOUSE . 12

CHAPTER III.
ISRAEL AND JUDAH, TO THE CLOSE OF OMRI'S DYNASTY . . 35

CHAPTER IV.
THE TWO KINGDOMS DURING THE DYNASTY OF JEHU . . 91

CHAPTER V.
THE TWO KINGDOMS, TO THE FALL OF THE ISRAELITE MONARCHY 117

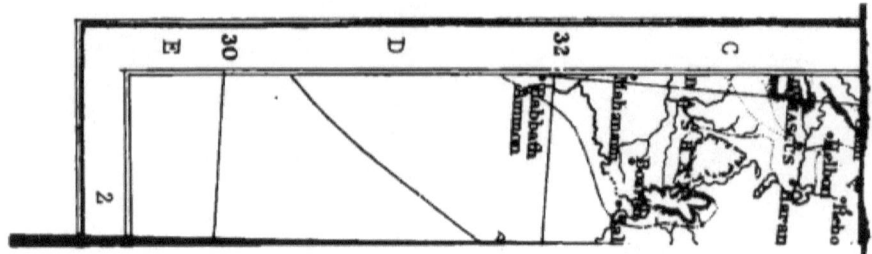

THE KINGDOMS OF ISRAEL AND JUDAH.

CHAPTER I.

THE DISRUPTION.

B.C. 975. From the establishment of monarchy 120 years; from the entrance of Israel into Canaan, 476 years.

GREAT national revolutions are sudden only in appearance. The thunderbolt may seem to have fallen from a clear sky; but unobserved elements of disturbance have long existed in the atmosphere, and have silently gathered strength for the decisive moment. Thus the catastrophe which rent in twain the Hebrew monarchy at the very height of its splendour might have been foreseen by political sagacity; and the arrogant folly of the young Rehoboam was but the spark which precipitated an inevitable explosion.

From the time when Jacob marked out JOSEPH as his best-beloved son, a certain ascendency over his

References and Authorities.

Existing elements of disturbance.

Gen. xxxvii. 3 Ascendency of Joseph and pretensions of Ephraim jealous brethren seemed the predestined lot of Rachel's elder child. The youthful dreams of Joseph, marvellously fulfilled as they had been in his later days, were naturally stored in remembrance by his descendants, as assuring their pre-eminence among the tribes. Among the prophetic blessings pronounced by Jacob on his death-bed the chief benediction was given to Joseph; and Moses, in his farewell to Israel on the banks of the Jordan, repeated and confirmed the declaration. Of the two sons of Joseph, again, EPHRAIM was marked out for the higher destiny. The dying Jacob "set Ephraim before Manasseh." "The seed of the younger brother," declared the patriarch, "shall become a multitude of nations;" and in like manner Moses spoke of the "ten thousands of Ephraim, and the thousands of Manasseh."

In the conquest of Canaan the tribe of Ephraim, though numerically inferior to almost all the rest, gave to the armies of Jehovah their illustrious leader, JOSHUA, the son of Nun. It was but natural that in the partition that followed, the fairest and richest portion of the land should fall to the same tribe. The limestone range called "Mount Ephraim," with its fair valleys and perennial streams, its pastures among the hills, with the corn-fields and orchards on their slopes, formed the rich inheritance of the two sons of Joseph; while, as half Manasseh was beyond the Jordan, the chief share both of territory and wealth on the western side was possessed by the descendants of the younger. The great historic shrines of Israel belonged to Ephraim. Bethel, where Jacob had dreamed in his flight, though apportioned by lot to Benjamin, was seized and held by the larger tribe. Shechem, where the patriarch had found a home beside "the well," was in the portion of Ephraim; so were Ebal and Gerizim, the hills of the blessing and the curse, with the tomb of Joshua in Timnath-serah, and Shiloh, where the tabernacle of the congregation was reared after the conquest of the land. *References and Authorities.* Gen. xxviii. 19; Josh. xvi. 1; xviii. 22; Judg. i. 22—25. Gen. xxxiii. 18; John iv. 5, 6. Josh. viii. 33. Josh. xxiv. 30.

Everything thus far seemed to mark out for this tribe the chief place in Israel; nor were the "men of Ephraim" slow to claim the privilege. Thus we find them taking Gideon to task because he called them not to go out to fight with him against the Midianites; while their indignation against Jephthah for a similar alleged neglect broke out into sanguinary strife. When the kingdom was established the supremacy seemed to pass for the time to Benjamin; but the sons of Joseph could hardly be jealous of the descendants of his favourite brother. No mention indeed is made of Ephraim in the days of Saul, but the tribe is included among those over which his son Ish-bosheth exercised a shadowy sovereignty for two years: the house of JUDAH however, "followed *David,*" and from this time the Divine choice was manifested. The king after Israel's own heart had proved wanting; the monarch "after God's own heart" was to establish a lasting throne. Thus also was the prediction of the dying Jacob to be fulfilled, "The sceptre shall not depart from Judah." Josh. xviii. 1. Jealousies of Ephraim. Judges viii. 1. Judges xii. 1—6. 1 Sam. ix. 21; Psalm lxviii. 27. 2 Sam. ii. 9, 10. Gen. xlix. 10

At first the great central tribe seemed to fall peaceably into the new order. When David was Ephraim during the reign of David.

ISRAEL AND JUDAH.

<small>References and Authorities.
1 Chron. xii. 30.
1 Chron. xxvii. 10, 14.
Ps. lxxviii. 67, 68.</small>

anointed king in Hebron, after the death of Ish-bosheth, there came of Ephraim two thousand eight hundred men to the solemn assembly of the tribes; and in the enumeration of his "chief captains" two Ephraimites are expressly mentioned. But the adoption of Jerusalem as the civil and ecclesiastical metropolis, thus at one blow depriving Shechem and Shiloh of

<small>Ps. lx. 7; cviii. 8.</small>

their former honours, could not but have roused much bitter resentment. The tribe in which "the strength" of Israel lay, would be ill disposed to submit to another tribe as "lawgiver." In accord, again, with the angry jealousy displayed of old against Gideon and Jephthah was the fierce remonstrance of the "men of Israel," when David returned to Jerusalem

<small>2 Sam. xix. 41—43.</small>

after Absalom's rebellion. "Why have our brethren the men of Judah stolen thee away? . . we have ten parts in the king; . . why then did ye despise us, that our advice should not be first had?" Sheba, son of Bichri, whose abortive sedition followed, though

<small>2 Sam. xx. 1, 21.</small>

a Benjamite, was "a man of Mount Ephraim." It was he who first raised the ominous cry, "Every man to his tents, O Israel." The attempt at insurrection was soon repressed, but the vindictive feeling remained. Very definitely and decidedly had Ephraim begun to "envy Judah."

<small>Solomon and Jeroboam.</small>

The earlier days of Solomon's reign, in their peaceful splendour, in the magnitude of his public works, and the extent of his commercial enterprise, gave no occasion for domestic broils. In the troubles, however, which marked the latter part of his reign, appears one personage destined to play a leading part in the succeeding disruption. This was JEROBOAM, a young Ephrathite, son of one Nebat,* dwelling with his widowed mother Zeruah, at a place, now unknown, named Zereda, in the mountains of their ancestral tribe. He is described as a "mighty man of valour;" he was one, no doubt, whose abilities and powers marked him out as fitted for the public service; Solomon may also have been glad to propitiate a member of the powerful and disaffected tribe.

<small>References and Authorities. 1 Kings xi. 26—40.</small>

Jeroboam seems first to have been employed on the fortifications of the Millo† beneath Mount Zion, and the capacity there displayed led the king to make him the taskmaster, revenue collector, or perhaps lieutenant-governor (for so the phrase is variously understood) of Ephraim, and its sister tribe Manasseh. What purposes of revolt the youthful statesman may have cherished while engaged in his employment we cannot tell. The office, whatever its details, would bring to light whatever extravagance or corruption had crept into the high places of the land; it would also reveal any secret disaffection which might threaten the ruin of the monarchy; and the prophet Ahijah of Shiloh, discerning the signs of the times, and no

<small>Ahijah's prophecy.</small>

---

* A tradition preserved by Jerome identifies Nebat with Shimei, David's reviler, who was of the house of Saul. Jeroboam would thus be allied with the earliest royal house of Israel, and would have hereditary reasons for enmity to the reigning family. Shimei was, however, a Benjamite, and was slain at the very commencement of Solomon's reign. It is scarcely necessary to point out that Zeruah is an entirely different word from Zeruiah, the name of David's sister.

† See note A on v. 27 at the end of this chapter.

doubt speaking by Divine inspiration, gave voice to Jeroboam's most secret thoughts in a bold prophecy of impending disruption.

References and Authorities.

Jeroboam was returning from one of his visits to Jerusalem, pondering, it may be, the corruptions and embarrassments of the court, perhaps with the cry of unwilling labourers still in his ears, when Ahijah met him and declared the oracle, rending his own garment into twelve pieces, ten of which he gave to Jeroboam as a symbol of the number of tribes which should revolt from Judah. The prediction, like Samuel's anointing of Saul and of David, was in the first instance private. Jeroboam and Ahijah "were alone in the field;" but it seems to have led to some overt act of rebellion on the part of Jeroboam. He "lifted up his hand against the king," but prematurely. Solomon discovered how powerful a rival had arisen to the house of David, and sought to kill Jeroboam, who fled to Egypt, placing himself under the protection of its king Shishak, now for the first time mentioned in the history of the Jews.

On the list of tribes, see chap. ii., p. 14.

Meantime king Solomon sank into his grave, and REHOBOAM, who, so far as appears from the history, was his *only* son, reigned in his stead. The public inauguration of the young monarch was appointed to take place at Shechem,—in itself a politic arrangement, as acknowledging that other tribes than Judah had a portion in the house of David, and restoring to the ancient capital something of its honour. Shechem also was central, and easily accessible, by the fords at Penuel, to the trans-Jordanic tribes.

Inauguration of Rehoboam.

1 Kings xii. 1.

In anticipation of the ceremony Jeroboam had returned from Egypt, prepared to vindicate the independence of the house of Joseph, and filled with that personal ambition which, since the prophecy of Ahijah, could not have slumbered in his mind. Naturally he took the head of the deputation which sought Rehoboam on behalf of all Israel, and the request presented was both just and moderate. Some, indeed, have doubted whether the allegation was strictly true,—whether, in fact, the burdensomeness of Solomon's reign had not been exaggerated. In one place we are expressly told that "of the children of Israel did Solomon make no bondmen," the heavier part of all his public works being assigned to the subject Canaanites. In this view it was an "ignorant impatience of taxation" that urged its claim, and the request for alleviation was but a pretext for revolt.

References and Authorities.

1 Kings ix. 22.

On the other hand, however, it is too clear that the luxuries of Solomon could not but have made enormous demands on the most willing of people, while the very extent and grandeur of his undertakings must have been oppressive in various ways. A heavy money tax had no doubt been imposed; and whilst such an impost is naturally hateful to all free nations, Israel, educated under the theocracy, had no primary conviction of the necessity of maintaining a royal house. The king had, however, a certain right to the services of his subjects, at first probably confined to military duty, and extended gradually and illegally to other descriptions of labour; and it was the oppressive extent of this forced feudal service that formed the

Measure of justice in the people's claim.

See 1 Kings iv. 7, 23.

Ewald, *History of Israel.*

<small>*References and Authorities.*</small> chief burden of Israel's complaint. To this was doubtless added indignation that the tributes of subject cities and the produce of increased foreign trade were swallowed up in maintaining the prodigal magnificence of the court, and produced no proportionate advance in the general prosperity of the country. At any rate, the people plainly saw that for their own defence the new king must be bound by those constitutional restrictions which, imposed upon the first two kings, seem to have been omitted at the accession of Solomon.

<small>Rehoboam's decision; the revolt.</small> For three days they were kept in suspense, the very delay indicating pretty plainly the mind of the young king. Prompt concession might have saved all; but the kingdom was doomed, and the senseless companions of Rehoboam, who imagined that a great people could be thus coerced, were but ministers of <small>1 Kings xii. 15.</small> a divine purpose. "The king hearkened not unto the people, for the cause was from the Lord." Again went forth the cry, "To your tents, O Israel!" and this time with dread significance. The long-cherished envy had at last culminated, and without a single blow the disruption was complete. So bloodless, indeed, was the revolution, that Rehoboam was deceived, and it was not until the stoning of his messenger opened his eyes that he fled to Jerusalem. Judah alone, with its associated tribes,* remained faithful to him, and thus the words of the prophet Ahijah were brought to their <small>1 Kings xi. 32.</small> sure fulfilment.

* See next chapter.

NOTES TO CHAPTER I.

References and Authorities.

A. Earlier History of Jeroboam.

This is contained only in the First Book of Kings (xi. 26—40). The Second Book of Chronicles introduces Jeroboam abruptly (x. 2), but expressly refers to the prophecy of Ahijah the Shilonite (x. 15).

1 Kings xi. 27. **Millo;** rather "the Millo," a word of unknown derivation, rendered in the LXX. "the citadel." It was probably an old Jebusite name for some part of the fortress of Zion. The works of Solomon here were undertaken in about the twenty-fifth year of his reign.

28. **The charge of the house of Joseph;** possibly the forced labour exacted from the tribes of Ephraim and Manasseh. Jeroboam would have to procure workmen, and to superintend their work.

29. *The rending of Ahijah's garment.* "The first instance," says the "Speaker's Commentary," "of that mode of delivering a divine message which became so common in later times, and which has been called 'acted parable.'"

33. **They have forsaken me.** Many of the people, as courtiers and others, had taken part in the idolatry of Solomon and his wives.

36. **A light,** or *lamp.* See Psa. cxxxii. 17. Emblem of continued prosperity. The lamp lighted every evening denotes a settled, peaceful home.

38. **A sure house,** on certain conditions which were unfulfilled; so that the house of Jeroboam soon became extinct.

40. **Shishak.** See note on chap. ii.; also Tuck's "First Three Kings of Israel," 1, 20.

B. Note on Jeroboam in the Septuagint.

The LXX. has a remarkable insertion in 1 Kings xii., which at once deranges the order of events, and gives to the history in many respects a new aspect and colouring. Jeroboam is represented as son of Sarira, a harlot, is made by Solomon superintendent of the forced labours of the tribe of Ephraim, and fortifies for him a city in Mount Ephraim, also named Sarira. Becoming rich and assuming an almost royal state, he is obliged

References and Authorities. to flee to Egypt to escape the wrath of the king. Shishak receives him cordially, and on Solomon's death detains him by giving him in marriage his own wife's sister. Upon the birth of his son Abijah he returns to Palestine and settles at Sarira, which he strongly fortifies. Abijah now falls sick, and Jeroboam's wife visits the prophet Ahijah (cap. xiv. 1—16). The child dies; Jeroboam goes to Shechem, whither he has gathered all the tribes of Israel, and here the prophetical announcement (cap. xi. 29—39) is made to him; the prophet, however, is not Ahijah, but Shemaiah the Enlamite. Then the events related in cap. xii. 5—24 are made to follow.

This passage conflicts with the Hebrew text in many important particulars:—(1) The time of the prophetical announcement to Jeroboam; (2) the person who made it; (3) the time of the illness and death of Abijah; (4) the ground of Jeroboam's original revolt; and (5) the ground of the sentence of extermination passed upon his family. Dean Stanley accepts the narrative as found in the Septuagint; but most Biblical critics, apparently with good reason, regard the ordinary account as of the higher authority.

C. Narrative of the Disruption.

This is given both in 1 Kings and in 2 Chronicles, and is plainly the same narrative, repeated with slight verbal differences.

1 Kings xii. and 2 Chron. x. *K.*, **dwelt in Egypt**; *Chr.*, **returned out of Egypt.** The LXX. has the latter phrase in both passages.

8. Grown up with him, trained for office by companionship with the young prince, as common in Eastern courts. According to 1 Kings xiv. 21, 2 Chron. xii. 13, Rehoboam was now forty-one years of age. If so, he was born before the accession of Solomon, which is improbable (see *Spk. Comm.*), as his mother Naamah was an Ammonite, and David would hardly have allowed his favourite son to marry into that heathen community. See also 2 Chron. xiii. 7, "young and tender-hearted." The likelihood is that the number has been corrupted by transcribers, and that for forty-one we should read *twenty-one.*

11. Scorpions; possibly a metaphorical expression for a scourge which would inflict the keenest possible sting. It is said by some that scourges armed with knots and spikes were so termed.

16. See to thine own house, David; *i. e.*, let the descendants of David henceforth confine themselves to their own tribe—that of Judah. Josephus interprets the words, "We only leave to Rehoboam the temple which his father built,"—an evident misreading.

17. The children of Israel, &c.; members of the ten tribes who had settled in the cities of Judah. To this number many were afterwards added, attracted to the southern kingdom by regard to the religion of their fathers (2 Chron. xi. 16).

References and Authorities.
1 Kings xii.
and
2 Chron. 1.

CHAPTER II.

THE TWO KINGDOMS, TO THE FALL OF JEROBOAM'S HOUSE.

B.C.	Israel.	Judah.
975	JEROBOAM Prophet *Ahijah*.	REHOBOAM Prophets, *Shemaiah Iddo*.
971		Invasion by Shishak.
958		ABIJAH OR ABIJAM.
	Great war. Battle of Mount Zemaraim.	
955		ASA.
954	NADAB	
952	Slain by BAASHA.	
	Dynasty of Jeroboam ends.	*Asa still reigning.*

---

§ 1.—THE TWO KINGDOMS.

THE covenant name of ISRAEL was from the first assumed by the kingdom of the ten tribes; whether owing to the pride of Ephraim, or by direct divine sanction, we have no means of knowing. Certain it is that the title was used from the very beginning of the disruption; and it appears to have been allowed to pass without question. Very possibly the house of David preferred their own tribal appellation to the more general name, the more distinctly to mark the fact that the crowning glory of the chosen people was the heritage of JUDAH. For the covenant was two-fold:—to "the house of Israel" belonged the promises in general; to "the house of Judah" the one promise of the CHRIST. Hence the secondary title, as it might seem to be, became that of greatest honour, and to be "a man of Judah"—a Jew—was a prouder claim than simply to belong to Israel. After the promise had been fulfilled, the name of Israel resumed its ancestral glory; and in the New Testament it expresses the highest honour of the covenant people; the word *Jew* denoting the national distinction in its widest sense, while the *Israelite* is "a member of the theocracy, and thus an heir of the promises." *References and Authorities.* *Jer. xxx. 31.* *The word Jew occurs only once before the captivity 2 Kings xvi 6. (xxv. 25.) In Nehemiah and Esther it is frequent.* *See Trench, N.T. Synonyms, § 39.*

The tribes which obeyed the call of Ephraim and Jeroboam are described as "ten." Some obscurity hangs over the enumeration, as the descendants of four of the sons of Jacob, and partially even those of five, are plainly excluded. *Thus the remnant of other tribes than that of Judah were termed Jews.*

Benjamin from the outset cast in its lot with Judah; the *Levites*, we are expressly told, left their allotted cities in the northern kingdom and came to Judah and Jerusalem; while the position of *Simeon* to the south of Judah, and of the half-tribe of *Dan* on the hills to the north-east, would effectually prevent *Chron. xi. 13, 14.*

those communities from joining themselves to the kingdom of Israel. Very few notices of the Simeonites occur in the later history; but so late as the days of Hezekiah a remnant of the once powerful tribe is found occupying their old abode in the south; while, on the other hand, the mention of the tribe on two occasions in connexion with Ephraim and Manasseh seems to show some affinity with the northern kingdom. The tribe had probably ceased to exist as a separate community, and the word of their great progenitor with respect to the brethren Levi and Simeon was fulfilled,—"I will divide them in Jacob, and scatter them in Israel." *

References and Authorities.
1 Chron. iv. 41-43.
2 Chron. xv. 9, xxxiv. 6.
Gen. xlix. 7.

Omitting, then, these four, the ten tribes must be enumerated thus, passing northward—

West of Jordan.	East of Jordan.
1. Ephraim.	8. Reuben.
2. W. Manasseh.	9. Gad.
3. Issachar.	10. E. Manasseh.
4. Zebulun.	
5. Asher.	
6. Naphtali.	
7. Dan (the northern half).	

* "It has often been pointed out how differently the same sentence was accomplished in the cases of the two tribes. Both were 'divided' and 'scattered.' But how differently! The dispersion of the Levites arose from their holding the post of honour in the nation, and being spread, for the purposes of education and worship, broadcast over the face of the country. In the case of Simeon the dispersion seems to have arisen from some corrupting element in the tribe itself, which first reduced its

The frontier of the kingdom is definable with some clearness, as shown in the map. Still there was always a belt of debatable land between the two kingdoms, the possession alternately of the stronger. Thus *Bethel*, at one period, fell into the hands of Judah, although for the most part held by the northern kingdom. *Ramah*, which was but five miles from Jerusalem, was taken and retaken by the rival powers. Passing eastward, we find that *Jericho* was rebuilt and fortified in the days of Ahab by a man of Bethel, from which we may conclude that the former city, like the latter, then belonged to Israel. On the west the boundary line joined the sea at about the northern extremity of Philistia. *References and Authorities.* Frontier.

2 Chron. xiii. 19.

1 Kings xv. 17, 21, 22, and 2 Chron. xvi. 1, 5, 6.
1 Kg. xvi. 34.

The extent of territory occupied by the twelve tribes at the death of Solomon is calculated by Kiepert at 12,810 English square miles, excluding the Philistine territory. Of this area Israel occupied about 9,375, and Judah 3,435 square miles. "Hence it appears that the whole area of Palestine was nearly equal to that of the kingdom of Holland, or that of the six northern counties of England (13,136 square miles). The kingdom of Judah was rather less than Northumberland, Durham, and Westmoreland (3,683 square miles); the kingdom of Israel was very nearly as large as Yorkshire, Lancashire, and Cumberland (9,453 square miles)." Extent of the territories.
Bible-Atlas, Berlin, 1850

---

members, and at last drove it from its allotted seat in the country—not, as Dan, because it could not, but because it would not stay,—and thus in the end caused it to dwindle and disappear entirely."—GEORGE GROVE, in "Dict. of Bible," Art. " Simeon."

ISRAEL AND JUDAH.

References and Authorities. Rev. R. W. Browne, Bib Dict. Art. "Israel." Populations.

The population of Israel may be reckoned from the number of fighting men whom Jeroboam was able to bring into the field. These, comprising men of twenty years old and upwards, are reckoned as 800,000, from which a population of at least three millions and a half may be inferred. At the same time, Abijah, king of Judah, commanded an aggregate army of 400,000, which, by a similar reckoning, would give at least 1,750,000 as, at that time, the population of the southern kingdom.* It would appear, however, that the latter was largely increased in succeeding generations, although the evident corruption of numerical statements in some passages makes a positive conclusion impossible.

2 Chron. xiii. 3.

See p. 28.

It is obvious that two kingdoms of so small an extent, often hostile to each other, and lying between great warlike nations, would be exposed to constant peril. Egypt, Syria, and the mighty Eastern power, were a perpetual menace to the very existence of the chosen race, and the whole history down to the final catastrophe shows a series of inroads upon the independence of the Hebrew monarchies. To a certain extent, the mutual jealousies of the heathen powers were the safeguard of Judah and Israel. Their land was an effectual barrier to the designs of Egypt upon Syria, or of Assyria and Babylon

* According to the census of 1871, the population of the six northern counties of England was 7,198,847, viz., Northumberland, Durham, and Westmoreland, 1,193,981; Yorkshire, Lancashire, and Cumberland, 6,004,866. The present population of all Syria is probably under 2,000,000, or about 40 persons to a square mile. See Bädeker's *Guide Book to Syria and Palestine*, p. 86.

upon Egypt. Its security was in a firm neutrality; and the alliance with one or the other of the surrounding nations was really more perilous than the common enmity of all. The remark is made here, as it is a key to much both of the history and of the connected prophecies.

References and Authorities.

§ 2.—ISRAEL UNDER THE DYNASTY OF JEROBOAM.

No sooner was Jeroboam settled in the kingdom than he devoted himself to its consolidation and defence. SHECHEM he selected as the capital; he also reconstructed the fortification—long ago destroyed by Gideon—at the important ford of PENUEL on the Jabbok, commanding the eastern tribes and the chief Jordan passes from that side. TIRZAH, the "city of delight," an old royal city of the Canaanites, destroyed by Joshua, was subsequently chosen by Jeroboam for his residence, and remained the chief abode of the Israelite kings until Omri built Samaria.

Measures of Defence.
Judges viii. 17.
Sol. Song vi. 4.
Josh. xii. 24.

It was, however, to the modification of the national worship that the chief aims of the new ruler were directed. So long as Jerusalem remained the gathering-place of the tribes it would plainly be impossible to contest the supremacy of Judah, while to build a temple in rivalry with that of Solomon would be as obviously futile. Jeroboam therefore took the audacious step of attempting to change, not only the place, but the method of divine worship. Instead of Jerusalem, he fixed upon Dan and Bethel,

Changes in National Worship.

at the two extremities of his kingdom, the former on the Syrian frontier, the latter on that of the kingdom of Judah. The worship, moreover, was to be that of "calves," a plain relapse into that form of Egyptian idolatry which had so fatally perverted the Israelites on their emancipation from the house of bondage. During Jeroboam's residence in Egypt he had no doubt become familiar with the symbols of Deity that were current in that land, and his purpose was not to introduce any new god to Israel, but to represent JEHOVAH under an external form. The sin of the Israelitish king therefore differed from the subsequent transgression of Ahab as the second commandment differs from the first. To have "other gods," as the Phœnician Baal, is one thing; to bow down to a "graven image," as the symbolic representation of the true God, is another. The latter was Jeroboam's crime, as it had been Aaron's. For the erring priest, when calling Israel to the adoration of the "golden calf," had expressly declared, "This is thy God that brought thee out of the land of Egypt," and had heralded his idolatrous rites by the proclamation, "To-morrow is a feast unto Jehovah." Jeroboam repeats the former announcement in the selfsame words. King and people forgot the awful warning then given to Israel, that the worship of God must be not only *exclusive*, but *spiritual*, and that no earthly form could symbolize Him whom man might not look upon and live. To maintain this spirituality in religion was an especial end of the Mosaic dispensation. Jeroboam proved himself unmindful of the main principle of the religion which he professed to honour, and so, as the sacred historians impressively reiterate, he "made Israel to sin."   *References and Authorities.* 1 Kings xv. 34; xvi. 19, 26; xxii. 52, &c.

The tribe of Levi, to its lasting honour, refused to abet the new worship; the Levites, therefore, with the priests, repaired from their respective cities to Jerusalem. The king accordingly instituted a new priesthood, and in further disregard of the divine ordinance, appointed his priests from the "ends of the people," that is, from all tribes and ranks indiscriminately. These priests were dedicated with the offering of "a bullock and seven rams," instead of "a bullock and two rams,"—according to the ancient statute; thus, even in comparatively small matters, marking the divergence from the old order: while a greater innovation still was introduced into the celebration of the Feast of Tabernacles; "the fifteenth day (or full moon) of the *eighth* month" being substituted for the fifteenth day of the *seventh* month. The alleged reason may have been that the harvest is later in the north than in the south of Palestine; but the principle was that of will-worship, Jeroboam devising the month, in the words of the sacred narrator, "out of his own heart."   Jeroboam's Priests. 1 Kings xii. 31; not precisely "the *lowest* of the people." Lev. viii. 2. Lev. xxiii. 34.

While celebrating this newly ordained festival at Bethel a strange portent happened. Suddenly there appeared a prophet from the southern land, well known to the people in that sacred character, although his name has perished, who apostrophising the altar itself, declared that on a future day it should be dese-   Testimony of the Prophet from Judah.

crated and its priests destroyed. He even designates by name the king by whom this would be accomplished, a circumstance with only one or two parallels throughout the Old Testament prophecies. The king, infuriated by the bold prediction, attempted to arrest the prophet, but his outstretched arm was for the moment paralysed, while the altar was rent as if by earthquake. Yet not even thus was Jeroboam deterred from his impious course. He may even have been emboldened in his wickedness by the terrible fate which soon overtook the prophet who had denounced him.* Like men in every age, he only too probably took occasion from the fall of the messenger to disregard the message. The true lesson would have been that "God is not mocked," and that if even a prophet was smitten for one act of disobedience, much more would punishment overtake the daring and hardened transgressor. The king disregarded the warning, and thus has left his name as a beacon through all the history, so that the worst of the kings are sufficiently described as followers of "Jeroboam the son of Nebat."

One gleam of light, soon quenched, shines in the palaces of Israel. Abijah, the beloved son of Jeroboam, bearing a name which shows that the king claimed to be still a worshipper of Jehovah, was smitten by sickness unto death. It is significant that in the sore distress which this calamity brought upon

---

* Josephus seems to identify this prophet with "Iddo the Seer," but this must be a mistake, as Iddo survived to the days of Abijah.

the royal household, it was the *mother* who set out *References and Authorities.*
to seek the prophet of God. In earlier days Ahijah
had been the counsellor of Jeroboam, and had assigned
the kingdom to him, and his posterity after him, on
condition of obedience to God's commandments.
The king has broken the covenant, and the blessing
seems vanishing from his home. Ahijah, still dwelling
at Shiloh, no doubt in stern if silent disapproval of
the proceedings at Dan and Bethel, may perhaps even
yet be prevailed upon to intercede with God for the
afflicted parents. Let the queen then seek him, not
as the spouse of a perjured king, but only as a
mother, broken-hearted at the prospect of losing her
child. For this purpose a disguise is assumed, which,
however, the seer penetrates at once. Ahijah must
be faithful, though at the cost of inflicting keenest
anguish upon the less guilty of the two. As Jeroboam will not himself come to hear, his queen must
listen to the stern words of rebuke and judgment.
He has sinned away his privilege; his dynasty
must fall, his son must die. Not the early piety and
bright promise of Abijah's youth, not the affections of
the people who hoped to have him as their king,
could save him; the prince's life is doomed; and after *Death of Abijah.*
him all would be dark night! In despair the queen
returned to Tirzah, the beautiful home which had now
no more charm for her; for "when she came to the
threshold of the door, the child died." "And all
Israel mourned for him."

Towards the close of Jeroboam's reign a great but *Attempt to crush Judah.*
ineffectual effort was put forth by him to break the

References and Authorities.

Jeroboam dies heart-broken.

power of Judah. This will be noticed in the succeeding section. He never recovered the tremendous failure; and though surviving it for three years, it was as a stricken, heart-broken man.

NADAB his son followed him on the throne of Israel. But the doom had gone forth; what Nadab might have been, or would have accomplished, had his years been lengthened, it is impossible for us to know. His beginnings seem to have been all evil, and he reigned for only two years. At the expiration of that time we find

Josh. xxi. 23.
1 Kings xvi. 15.

him besieging Gibbethon, an old Levitical city once belonging to southern Dan, but now and long after held by the Philistines. In the course of the siege

1 Kings xvi. 2. "exalted out of the dust."

the king was murdered in a conspiracy, of which the head was BAASHA, a soldier of lowly origin, belonging to the comparatively obscure tribe of Issachar. The assassination of Nadab was followed, in Oriental fashion, by that of his whole house. The great Ephraimite family became extinct; and Baasha, now raised to the throne, was an unconscious instrument in fulfilling the doom which the prophet of Shiloh in the name of the Lord had declared to the wife of Jeroboam.

§ 3.—The Kingdom of Judah during Jeroboam's Dynasty.

References and Authorities.

There are some singular coincidences in the histories of the rival Hebrew kings. The word JEROBOAM means "Whose people is many;" while REHOBOAM signifies "Enlarger of the people"—a futile prophecy, or an empty boast. It is remarkable, too, that each monarch named his son *Abijah*—"Jehovah is my father,"—both thus claiming, as has been already noted in the case of Jeroboam, a part in the ancient covenant. That part was especially assured to the line of David; but the unworthy grandson of that great king was obstinately disposed to throw away the privilege. His reign was one of unsettlement and disaster. From the first his throne seemed to be threatened on all sides. But at the outset he had assumed the aggressive. When returning discomfited from Shechem he proceeded to collect a great army, 180,000 strong, to bring back the revolted tribes to the house of David. But the prophet Shemaiah, in the name of God, denounced the enterprise; on which the army voluntarily disbanded, and the attempt to reconquer Israel was for a while abandoned; no friendly relations, however, being established between the two monarchies until after renewed and terrible conflicts. Between Rehoboam and Jeroboam "there was" a standing "war all the days of their lives." Abijam and Jeroboam broke into open hostility; and after the great battle of

Names of the two kings.

The unworthy heir of the covenant.

Abortive attempt to re-conquer Israel.

References and Authorities. Mount Zemaraim, the strife continued in a series of petty feuds all along the frontier of the kingdom.

Rehoboam's fortresses. Forbidden to attack Israel in force, and fearing the possibilities of an alliance between Jeroboam and his old patron, Shishak, Rehoboam addressed himself after the disbanding of his army to the construction of a series of fortresses, chiefly south and south-west of Jerusalem. A glance at the rough diagram annexed will show, more vividly than any description, the quarter from which attack was feared. Every road and pass by which the forces of Egypt could approach seems to have been commanded, although no fortresses were set up in the direction of the Israelite frontier; while the defences were in some measure securities against Moab on one side and Philistia on the other.

2 Chron. xi. 6—10.

Rehoboam's decline. These proceedings seem to have occupied three years, during which the kingdom was prosperous. That accession of priests and Levites to which reference has been already made, with that of many devout Israelites, driven from their homes by the impieties of Jeroboam, would deepen the religious character of the nation; and once more Jehovah seemed to favour His chosen people. But when the stress of enterprise had passed, and the king was able to seek luxurious ease, the temptations which had so fatally prevailed over Solomon achieved an easier victory over Rehoboam. First we are told that he had "eighteen wives and sixty concubines;" next, in impressive sequence, that he and all his people with him "forsook the law of Jehovah." From

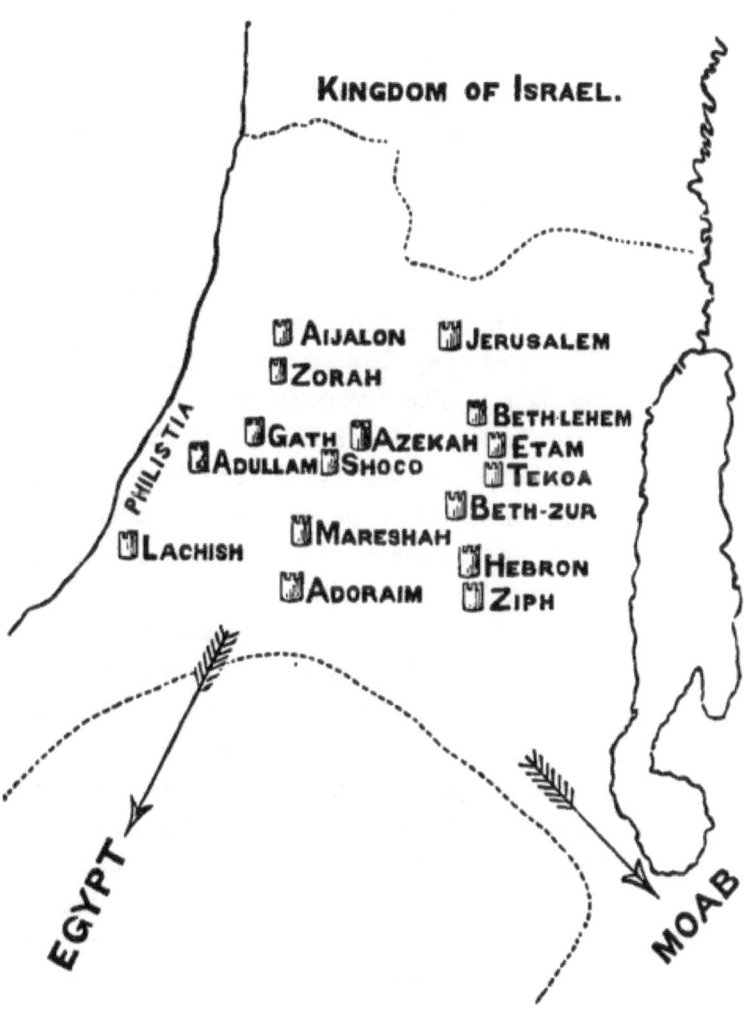

SKETCH MAP OF REHOBOAM'S FORTRESSES.

glimpses given us of the idolatry into which Judah unhappily fell, we infer that it was even worse than that of Jeroboam. The licentious worship of Ashtoreth was revived, with "all the abominations" of the Canaanites. Luxury, sensuality, apostasy,— such was the easy gradation; and the punishment was swift and tremendous.

<small>*References and Authorities.*
Pagan idolatry.
1 Kings xv. 22—24.
"The grove."</small>

Rehoboam had not been five years upon the throne when his dreaded enemy, Shishak, at the head of an immense army of Libyans, Arabs, and Ethiopians swept in a sudden wave of invasion over the land. The fortresses which Rehoboam had reared in his way were easily crushed, and the hosts of Shishak soon environed Jerusalem. Resistance would have been hopeless; the despairing chiefs of Judah took counsel of Shemaiah the prophet, by the power of whose faithful words they were led to humble themselves before God; and Shishak was induced to spare the people on condition of their becoming vassals to Egypt. At the same time the proud invader demanded, as the price of his withdrawal, the golden treasures with which Solomon had enriched the temple. Rehoboam had no choice but to comply. "Shields of brass" were made to replace the "shields of gold" which had heretofore been stored in the sanctuary and borne in the temple processions: the pageants were continued, and very possibly the imitation served with the multitude as well as the lost reality.

<small>Invasion by Shishak. See Note D. Lubims and Sukkiims, tribes to the west and east of Egypt respectively. Ethiopians to the south.</small>

<small>"Two hundred targets of beaten gold," 2 Chron. ix.15.</small>

The rest of Rehoboam's reign appears to have been uneventful; the main points recorded being the

<small>End of Rehoboam's reign.</small>

constant ruthless strife between himself and Jeroboam, and the growing tendencies to idolatry on the part of sovereign and people. The "grove" worship was still maintained throughout the land, but there were here and there indications of better things. "There was yet some good," writes the inspired chronicler, "in Judah." God did "not utterly take His lovingkindness" from the grandson of David, nor "suffer His faithfulness to fail."

References and Authorities.

Ps. lxxxix. 30—33.

Of Rehoboam's numerous wives, the three favourites were descendants of Jesse. The first was *Maachah*, granddaughter of Absalom by his daughter Tamar, who seems to have been married to one Uriel, of Gibeah; the second was *Mahalath*, daughter of Jerimoth, one of the sons, apparently, of David's old age; the third was *Abihail*, a descendant of Eliab, the eldest son of Jesse. Of these wives, Maachah, the latest espoused, was the best beloved; and her son ABIJAH, or ABIJAM, was designated as heir to the kingdom. The latter form is given in the Kings, the other in the Chronicles. The prince was no doubt originally named Abijah (Jehovah my father); but afterwards Abijam, to dissociate the divine name from the designation of so ungodly a sovereign. In character he was a voluptuary; for the last time we have mention of a numerous seraglio of "fourteen wives," by whom the king had "twenty-two sons, and sixteen daughters." After a reign of three years he sank to the tomb, protected only, says the historian, who discloses the divine meaning of the outward facts, "for David's sake."

Wives of Rehoboam.

Called also *Michaiah.*
2 Chr. xiii. 2.

Accession of Abijam.

His character.

One great event, however, marked the reign of Abijam. The smouldering hostility between the two kingdoms broke into fierce and sudden flame. Which of the two kings was the aggressor is unknown. It is possible that the wily Jeroboam had waited for the death of his old rival to strike, as he thought, a decisive blow at Jerusalem; or else Abijam, in the ardour of youth, may have aspired to reconquer the northern tribes to the house of David. What is certain is that both kingdoms were well prepared, and that all their resources were brought into the field. The numbers specified have appeared to many expositors incredible; it has even been supposed that copyists have multiplied the figures on both sides by ten. This assumption, however, we are by no means driven to adopt. The occasion was a great crisis; the old Israelite monarch and the youthful king of Judah put forth their utmost power. It was upon Mount Zemaraim that the decisive conflict took place. The locality cannot be identified; it was plainly on the southern side of Bethel, and yet was in Mount Ephraim, the lowest spurs of which extended some few miles into the territory of Judah. A city of the name is mentioned among the possessions of Benjamin.

Before the battle Abijam uttered a manifesto— extraordinary as coming from him,—in which he rested the whole case of Judah on its allegiance to Jehovah, and denounced the will-worship of Jeroboam. The principles of this famous address were sound; but in enunciating them Abijam must have strangely forgotten the Ashtoreth-worship and Canaanite abominations which defiled the land of Judah. Or had he in those early days of his reign some half-formed purpose to uproot these evils? We cannot tell. His bold declaration, "JEHOVAH is our God, and we have not forsaken Him" must either have pointed to some such design, or it was an impious boast. Very decisive was the victory of Judah. An ambush set by Jeroboam entirely failed. His mighty host, pressing on all sides around Rehoboam's army, was smitten with sudden panic, and fled so wildly that the latter had nothing to do but to pursue and slay. Half a million of Israelites are said to have been slain, perhaps including all who perished in the war and the sieges that followed. *Bethel* fell for a time beneath the Davidic dominion, with the unknown border-towns of *Jeshanah* and *Ephrain*; and the supremacy of Judah remained unquestioned through the remainder of Jeroboam's reign, as well as in the troubled times of his immediate successors.

<small>*References and Authorities.*</small>

The true character of Abijam unhappily showed itself soon after this eventful war; and the great opportunity for reformation which his victory had secured fell into the hands of his youthful son and successor, ASA, whose wise and prosperous reign had scarcely begun, when the worn-out dynasty of Jeroboam fell by the hand of Baasha, the fierce soldier of the tribe of Issachar.

<small>Accession of Asa.</small>

NOTES ON CHAPTER II.

A. PARALLEL PASSAGES AND SEPARATE ACCOUNTS.

Rehoboam's early purpose to invade Israel, 1 Kings xii. 21—24; 2 Chron. xi. 4: apparently the same document.

Impieties of Jeroboam, 1 Kings xii.; xiii. 34, only.

Early years of Rehoboam's reign, 2 Chron. xi. 5—23 only.

Steps of Judah towards apostasy, 1 Kings xiv. 22—24; 2 Chron. xii. 1.

INVASION BY SHISHAK.

Of this notable event two accounts are given; that in the Chronicles containing all that in the Kings, with additions.

1 Kings xiv. 25—28.

Kings.   "And it came to pass in the fifth year of king Rehoboam, that Shishak king of Egypt came up against Jerusalem; and he took away the treasures of the house of the Lord, and the treasures of the king's house; he even took away all: and he took away all the shields of gold which Solomon had made. And king Rehoboam made in their stead brazen shields, and committed them unto the hands of the chief of the guard, which kept the door of the king's house. And it was so, when the king went into the house of the Lord, that the guard bare them, and brought them back into the guard chamber."

2 Chronicles xii. 2—12.

Chronicles.   "And it came to pass, that in the fifth year of king Rehoboam, Shishak king of Egypt came up against Jerusalem, because they had transgressed against the Lord, with twelve hundred chariots, and threescore thousand horsemen: and the people were without number that came with him out of Egypt; the Lubims, the Sukkiims, and the Ethiopians. And he took the fenced cities which pertained to Judah, and came to Jerusalem.

"Then came Shemaiah the prophet to Rehoboam, and to the princes of Judah that were gathered together to Jerusalem because of Shishak, and said unto them, Thus saith the Lord, Ye have forsaken me, and therefore have I also left you in the hand of Shishak. Whereupon the princes of Israel and the king humbled themselves; and the said, The Lord is righteous.

"And when the Lord saw that they humbled themselves, the *References and Authorities.* word of the Lord came to Shemaiah, saying, They have humbled themselves; therefore I will not destroy them, but I will grant them some [or, a little while] deliverance; and my wrath shall not be poured out upon Jerusalem by the hand of Shishak. Nevertheless they shall be his servants; that they may know my service, and the service of the kingdoms of the countries.

2 Chron. xii. continued.

"So Shishak king of Egypt came up against Jerusalem, and took away the treasures of the house of the Lord, and the treasures of the king's house; he took all: he carried away also the shields of gold which Solomon had made. Instead of which king Rehoboam made shields of brass, and committed them to the hands of the chief of the guard, that kept the entrance of the king's house. And when the king entered into the house of the Lord, the guard came and fetched them, and brought them again into the guard chamber. And when he humbled himself, the wrath of the Lord turned from him, that he would not destroy him altogether: and also in Judah things went well [or, and yet in Judah there were good things]."

Abijah, or Abijam, his accession, 1 Kings xv. 1, 2; 2 Chron. xiii. 1, 2. On his mother's name, see p. 27

Character of Abijam, 1 Kings xv. 3—6 only. **His war with Jeroboam**, 2 Chron. xiii. 2—22 only. **His death**, 1 Kings xv. 7, 8; 2 Chron. xiv. 1.

Illness and death of Abijah, son of Jeroboam, 1 Kings xiv. 1—18 only.

Jeroboam's death, Reign of Nadab, and Conspiracy of Baasha, 1 Kings xiv. 19, 20; xv. 25—28, 31 only.

Accession of Asa, 1 Kings xv. 9, 10; 2 Chron. xiv. 1. On the "mother" of Asa, see chap. iii.

B. THE IDOLATRY OF JEROBOAM.

It is necessary to discriminate all through the history of the Israelites between the two forms of idolatry to which at different eras they were prone. The one was the forsaking Jehovah for the "gods of the nations," especially Baal and Ashtoreth, the Phœnician deities. Into this fearful sin Rehoboam fell (1 Kings xiv. 23), where the word translated "groves" denotes the image (*asherah*) of the goddess Ashtoreth. Compare what is said of

Two forms of Idolatry.

References and Authorities. Solomon's later years, chap. xi. 33. It is not certain that Jeroboam was *wholly* clear from this form of paganism (chap. xiv. 15); but his chief transgression was in his adopting the *second* form of idolatry, *i. e.*, the attempt to represent the true God under material forms. Dean Stanley even says of Jeroboam that "to keep the first commandment he broke the second," doing too much honour perhaps to the king's good intentions. It has also been suggested that Jeroboam, while adopting the Egyptian symbol, had also in mind the cherubim in the temple at Jerusalem, where the form of "an ox" was in part employed. Two hundred years after Jeroboam's time, the "calves" were still the objects of adoration in Israel (Hos. xiii. 2; viii. 5, 6). "That of Dan was carried away by Tiglath-pileser (2 Kings xv. 29); that of Bethel ten years afterwards by Shalmaneser (2 Kings xvii. 5, 6)." (F. W. FARRAR in *Smith's Dictionary*; PRIDEAUX, "Connexion," I. 15.

C. THE PROPHET FROM JUDAH.

Dean Stanley. "Who," says Dean Stanley, "was this mysterious prophet He has been called by many names,—Joam, according to Epiphanius; Abdadinai, according to Clement; Jadon, according to Josephus. We can hardly mistake in the last of these names the Grecised form of Iddo the seer. He was the author of a book of genealogies, as well as of histories of the reigns of Solomon, of Abijam, and of Jeroboam; and it adds to the impressiveness of the warning if we may suppose that it came from the chief prophet of the time. The motives of the "prophet from Bethel" are so obscurely given in the sacred narrative, and so differently related in the tradition of Josephus,[*] as almost to defy our scrutiny. He seems to be one of those mixed characters, true to history and human nature, which perpetually appear among the sacred persons of the Old Testament, moved by a partial wavering inspiration; aiming after good, yet failing to attain it; full of genuine tender admiration for the prophet, of whose death he had been the unwilling cause, the mouthpiece of truths which he himself but faintly understood."

[*] "Josephus (Ant. viii., 9, § 1) describes the elder prophet as moved by jealousy, and as explaining away to Jeroboam the miracles that attended the Judæan prophet. 'The king's arm was fatigued, the altar fell because it was new.' In Josephus, the divine warning of 1 Kings xiii. 20, 21 came direct to the younger prophet."

Mr. Keble (*Christian Year*, eighth Sunday after Trinity) has *References and Authorities.* well brought out some of the chief lessons of the narrative, although he seems to mistake the nature of the idolatry practised at Bethel.

> "Where angels down the lucid stair
> Came hovering to our sainted sires,
> Now, in the twilight, glare
> The heathen's wizard fires."

D. SHISHAK.

The reign of this monarch, Sheshenk or Sheshonk of the Egyptian monuments, offers the earliest *data* for ascertaining the comparative chronology of the Hebrew monarchs. The first year of Shishak corresponds to the twenty-sixth of Solomon, and therefore the fifth year of Rehoboam would fall in about the twentieth of Shishak. The expeditions of this king are sculptured on the wall of the great temple of El Karnak, Shishak being depicted as leading to the god a train of captives with shields on their breasts containing the names of their respective nations. "Amongst these the student can readily recognise certain well-known Scripture names, which have been read as follows :—' Land of *Mahanma*,' which Rosellini considers to be the *Mahanaim* of Gen. xxxii. 2, an ancient city belonging to the tribe of Gad ; 'land of *Baitaurhia*,' supposed to be the same as the two *Beth-horons* which Solomon fortified, according to 2 Chron. viii. 5 ; ' land of *Maktu*,' interpreted as the *Megiddo* of 2 Kings xxiii. 29, where three centuries later Josiah, king of Judah, was defeated by another king of Egypt, who is mentioned as Pharaoh Necho. The fourth and most interesting name which the genius of Champollion detected is that of the KINGDOM OF JUDAH, commonly but erroneously read as *Judah Melek*, which could only be rendered literally as Judah King, whereas the final hieroglyph, being the determination of a country, proves beyond all doubt that it means, not the reigning king, but the *kingdom* of Judah, which Pharaoh Shishak boasted of having subdued, and which exactly harmonizes with what Scripture records concerning his capture of Jerusalem."—*Church Quarterly Review*, July, 1876, art. "The Ancient Egyptians." The writer adds that he " possesses a photograph of this magnificent monument, recording Pharaoh Shishak's victories over his enemies.

References and Authorities. The figure of the King, as large as life, surrounded by inscriptions as legible as if they were done but yesterday (their real age being nearly 3,000 years), and amongst them the captive bearing on his breast the name of 'the kingdom of Judah' (this is the third figure in the list on a level with the king's knee), present a sight of no ordinary interest to the Biblical student. Copies of several of these figures are painted on the walls of the Egyptian Court in the Crystal Palace."

See also Dr. Manning's *Land of the Pharaohs*, p. 124, for a representation of the Karnak Temple wall.

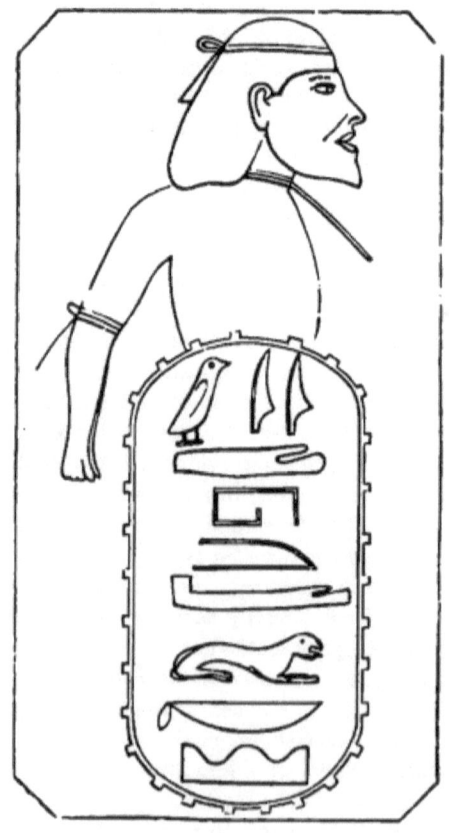

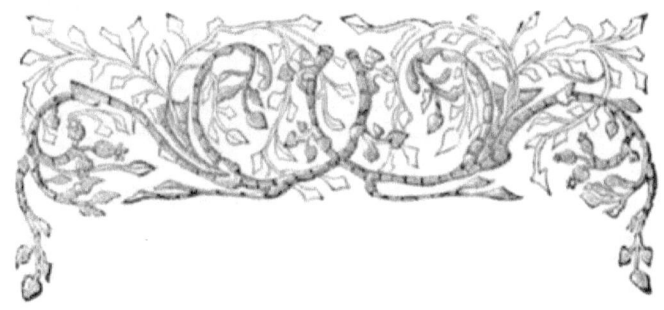

CHAPTER III.

ISRAEL AND JUDAH TO THE CLOSE OF OMRI'S DYNASTY.

B.C.	Israel.	Judah.

953	BAASHA	ASA reigning
		Great Cushite invasion
		Prophets—*Oded*
		         Azariah
		         Hanani
		         Jehu

930	ELAH	
929	ZIMRI	
925	OMRI—Civil War with Tibni	

918	OMRI alone
	AHAB
	    Prophets—*Elijah*
	            Micaiah	

914		JEHOSHAPHAT
	Alliance between the kingdoms.	
898	AHAZIAH Prophet—*Elisha*	Prophets—*Eliezer*
896	JEHORAM	*Jahasiel*
889		JEHORAM
885		AHAZIAH
884	Jehoram and Ahaziah slain.	
	Accession of JEHU	Usurpation of ATHALIAH

§ I. THE KINGDOM OF ISRAEL TO THE ACCESSION OF AHAB.

References and Authorities.
Baasha. Attempt to fortify Ramah. Probably about the 13th year of Baasha's reign.

The chief occurrence in the reign of BAASHA was an act of aggression against Judah, suppressed by king Asa with politic promptness. Bethel had fallen for the time under the power of the southern kingdom; and to make amends for the loss, as well as to secure a stronger position, the king of Israel seized upon Ramah, only five miles from Jerusalem, and began to construct fortifications. Asa seems to have felt himself powerless to hinder the design; but fully apprehending the importance of decisively thwarting it, he sent large subsidies from the remaining treasures of the court and temple in Jerusalem to Benhadad, king of Syria, now first mentioned in the sacred history, to induce him to make a counter-movement against Israel. The scheme was successful. Benhadad attacked the northern cities of Dan and Naphtali; Baasha was compelled to hurry his forces to their defence; the works at Ramah were stopped, and Asa marched triumphantly in, dismantling the fortress, and employing its materials in strengthening the defences of Gibeah and Mizpah.

Baasha's wickedness.
Jehu. See 2 Chron. xix. 3. (thirty years after) xx. 34.

All other details of Baasha's reign are lost, save that he continued in the evil courses of Jeroboam, and was rebuked, with stern denunciation, by the youthfu prophet Jehu, the son of Hanani, of the kingdom of Judah. It is observable that the assassination of Nadab is declared to be one of the crimes on account of which Baasha and his house were doomed. Yet the king's elevation "out of the dust" was providentially ordered; and had not he, like Jeroboam, been false to the purposes of his high calling, he would have prospered. "*My people* Israel" is still the divine designation of the revolted tribes, as truly as of those who maintained their allegiance to the house of David.

References and Authorities.

The "Book of the Chronicles of the Kings of Israel," which contains the further record of Baasha's life, is wholly lost. After a reign of four-and-twenty years he was succeeded by ELAH, his son, who soon met a fate curiously resembling that by which the son of Jeroboam had fallen; only the murder was wrought, not in the field of warfare, but in the house of revelry. ZIMRI, one of his generals, was the author of the deed, and immediately grasped the sovereignty, which, however, he retained for only a week. The army, again gathered before Gibbethon, where Nadab had been assassinated six-and-twenty years before, was not disposed to acquiesce in the self-elevation of Zimri, and proclaimed its own commander-in-chief, Omri, as king in room of Elah. Zimri made an unsuccessful endeavour to defend himself in Tirzah, which had remained the capital of Israel since the days of Jeroboam; and when the city was taken, withdrew into the palace, set it on fire over his own head, and perished miserably. So fell the beautiful city; and though it was for ten years longer the nominal metropolis, it was plain that the seat of power must be transferred to another spot.

Elah.

Compare the death of Sardanapalus.

It was not without a struggle that OMRI obtained possession of the throne. A new pretender arose—one

Omri and Tibni.

Tibni, of whom nothing further is known, but who seems to have been the choice of the people, as Omri was of the army. The struggle continued for four years; in the end, the army, as might be expected, was triumphant: "Tibni died, and Omri reigned." The new king settled at first in Tirzah, like his predecessors; but military sagacity led him to seek a stronger position for the capital; and as Shechem was probably considered not sufficiently near the centre of the kingdom, he fixed upon a hill to the north, almost unequalled in its natural advantages, the property of one Shemer, from whom he purchased it for two talents of silver. A great compliment was paid to the former owner by the retention of his name in the form *Shimron*, or *Samaria*. Perhaps this was one of the conditions of the bargain; in any case, "Shemer's hill" became the metropolis of Israel, and the name in succeeding ages was taken to designate the district and its inhabitants.

Travellers and geographers have vied one with another in describing the strength and beauty of this fortress city. It is a perfect natural citadel. "The verdant valley which breaks through the mountains westward between Ebal and Gerizim spreads out after three or four miles into a broad circular basin five or six miles in diameter, and bounded on every side by beautiful mountains. From the rich plains of this glorious valley, enclosed by an amphitheatre of mountains, and near to the western side, rises a very high and steep hill, affording a position of impregnable strength, and of almost unapproachable loveliness. About midway up the ascent the hill is

SAMARIA.

surrounded by a narrow terrace of level ground, like a belt, below which the roots of the hill spread off more gradually into the valleys. This was the hill which belonged to one Shemer, and which Omri bought of him for about seven hundred pounds."

Kitto, D.B.S., Week 45, p. 194.

The reign of Omri, including the time of the struggle with his rival Tibni, lasted for twelve years. Nothing more is known of his history, save that he not only "followed Jeroboam," but seems to have enjoined idolatrous usages by law. The "statutes of Omri," of which the prophet Micah speaks, were evidently some royal decree to enforce that which Jeroboam had upheld by example and allurement. It was reserved for Ahab to introduce to Israel those fouler forms of idolatry which had already perverted Rehoboam and his sons, but from which, under the rule of Asa, the southern kingdom had been wholly purged. The rival monarchies, however, appear to have subsisted side by side in peace, though not in friendship. The northern power of Syria, once the dangerous ally of Judah, was the avowed foe of Israel; and though we are not told directly of any further attacks by Benhadad, the fact that Ramoth-gilead had passed into his hands shows how aggressive, as well as formidable, was the growing power of Damascus.

On the present condition of Samaria. See Keith, Prophecy, ch. v. pp. 249—254.

Annotated par. Bible.

A city of refuge. Deut. iv. 43. Josh. xx. 8. See 1 Kings xx. 34, xxii 3. When taken by Syria we are not informed.

Before proceeding to the history of Omri's son and successor it will be convenient to review the reign of the one Judæan king who had remained, through all these changes of Israel's dynasty, upon the throne of David.

§ 2. Asa.

References and Authorities.

Asa, grandson of Rehoboam, is noteworthy, first as a religious reformer, and then as the valiant defender of his kingdom against two formidable invasions. His reign was long as well as glorious. He ascended the throne in the closing year of Jeroboam; he witnessed the brief career of Nadab, the longer reign of Baasha, the hapless course of Elah, the usurpation and speedy death of Zimri, the struggle between Omri and Tibni, the accession of the former to undisputed sovereignty, his life and death, and the commencement of king Ahab's reign. Strange is the contrast between the convulsions which rent the northern kingdom, and the unbroken prosperity of the southern. The inspired historian assigns the reason: "Asa's heart was perfect with the Lord all his days." Not that he was faultless; his self-sufficiency, on at least two occasions, is recorded, and sternly blamed: by "perfection" we are to understand steadfastness of attachment to the true faith.

Contrast between the two kingdoms.

In all probability Asa was very young when called to reign. Should the view previously given be sustained that Rehoboam was but twenty-one years old when his youthful indiscretion rent the kingdom in twain, it is clear that now, at the distance of less than twenty years, Rehoboam's grandson must have been comparatively a child. How his education was conducted we can only conjecture. Abijam, his father, notwithstanding his vices, is shown by his remarkable address recorded in the Chronicles

See p. 10.

References and Authorities.

to have been, at least on occasion, a zealous admirer of the Levitical order : it is probable therefore on all accounts that the training of the youthful prince was entrusted to the priesthood. We meet also with another court personage, now for the first time appearing in the history, but evidently wielding, as usual in Oriental courts, a special prerogative. This is the "king's mother;" or, in the present instance, more strictly his grandmother, Maachah, the descendant of Absalom. Where polygamy is the habit of the court, the position of king's wife is precarious ; and she who may prove to have been but the favourite of a season cannot properly be styled "the queen." This honour therefore naturally belongs to the royal mother, who in some Eastern courts even exercises authority over the king her son. But Maachah was an idolatress after the corrupt Phœnician fashion ; she had made a "horror" (so runs the original) as an object of worship ; and one of the earliest acts of her grandson was to depose her from her queenly dignity.

So, in Turkey, the Sultana Validé.

He has been compared to Edward the Sixth.

It was an earnest of the stern resolution with which Asa addressed himself to the extirpation of heathen observances from the land of Judah. Of the foul Canaanite idolatries which his fathers had introduced, he made short work. Images and altars were destroyed, and the high places were dismantled. Such, at least, is the declaration of the Chronicles, while from the Kings we learn that with some inconsistency the king allowed those high places which were dedicated to the service of Jehovah to remain ; thus infringing the exclusive claim of Jerusalem to the altar rites.

The permission, whether deliberate and politic, or only weak, is imputed to Asa as a defect, which did not invalidate the sincerity and truthfulness of his devotion to the God of Israel. *References and Authorities.*

At what time in the reign of Asa the land was menaced by the great invasion of Zerah we are not explicitly informed. We read, however, on the one hand, that Judah was at peace for ten years from the young king's accession; while, on the other, the attack of Baasha, to which reference has already been made, occurred in or about the fifteenth year of Asa's reign. We have thus a limit of five years within which the invasion of Zerah must have taken place. For some such attack the king and people had been sedulously preparing. While urging forward the revival of religion throughout the land, attention had been given to the reconstruction of the fortresses which had fallen before Shishak, and to the enrolment of an army, which at the time of Zerah's attack was 580,000 strong. Judah and Benjamin furnished the force in nearly equal proportions, the smaller tribe having fast gained upon the larger, no doubt from the rapid growth of Jerusalem. *Zerah, "the Ethiopian."*

Judah 300,000; Benjamin 280,000.

The nationality of Zerah, the new enemy of Judah, must be pronounced a little uncertain. He is termed a "Cushite," a word that may denote Arabian tribes, though more usually standing for the Ethiopians south of Egypt. That a force from the latter country is intended has been argued from the mention of "chariots," as well as from the order of retreat of the routed army, from Mareshah to Gerar, *Gen. x. 7* in the direction of Egypt. In the absence of any strong reason to the contrary we may assume that "Cush" bears in this record its ordinary meaning, and that Zerah was either a king of Egypt or a southern potentate in alliance with him. The army was enormous—the largest of which we read in Scripture. Its base of operations seems to have been the district of Gerar, where the towns were under Egyptian sway. The vast unwieldy host advanced to Zephathah, the "Watch tower," in the neighbourhood of Mareshah, one of Rehoboam's fortresses dismantled by Shishak, restored by Asa. Details of the great battle that ensued have not been given. It is the only instance in all the annals of Judah of a victorious encounter in the field with any first-class heathen power in full force. For the victory of Jehoshaphat was not won by arms, and the destruction of Sennacherib's army was by "an angel of the Lord"; and on "the one other occasion on which they took the field, which was under Josiah against Necho, their boldness issued in a most disastrous defeat." The great point on which the inspired narrator fixes attention is the prayer of Asa before the battle. Never was appeal to God more beautiful in its simple faith; never was answer more manifest and decisive given by the Lord of hosts. Judah was triumphant; the myriads of Egypt and Ethiopia were driven backward upon Gerar. Nor were they suffered there to rally: this district was itself re-occupied by the victorious Hebrews, who gathered "exceeding much spoil," and returned in triumph to Jerusalem. The

Marginal notes:

References and Authorities. See diagram, p. 25.

Usarken I. third king of Egypt after Shishak. See art. ZERAH, in Smith's Dict. Bible.

"A thousand thousand," or a million, no doubt including all camp followers.

Smith's Dict., as above.

Speaker's Comm. 2 Chron. xiv. 12.

blow for the time was decisive, and it was three hundred years before any Egyptian force again menaced Jerusalem. *References and Authorities*

In classic days we are told that in the triumphal procession the conquering hero was accompanied in his car by one whose duty it was to moderate the exultation of the hour by whispering ever and anon, "*Man, remember thou art mortal.*" Nobler was the testimony borne before king Asa, at the head of his victorious thousands, by the prophet of the most high God, who came forth to meet them at the gates of Jerusalem. Azariah, the son of Oded, appearing here in the narrative for the first and last time, rejoices, as well he may, in the divine favour shown to his people; but with his congratulation blends the tone of solemn warning, "*The Lord is with you while ye be with Him; and if ye seek Him, He will be found of you; but if ye forsake Him, He will forsake you.*" Well if such thoughts could always find a place in the hour of victory! In accord with the prophet's appeal new vigour was thrown into the work of religious reformation. "The strangers out of Ephraim and Manasseh, and out of Simeon" marvelled at the godly zeal as much as they must have done at the mighty victory, and flocking from their own land, that was sinking deeper and deeper into idolatry, hasted to exchange the rule of Baasha for that of Asa. At or about the feast of Pentecost, in the fifteenth year of Asa's reign, a great festival was celebrated in Jerusalem, to which as in happier times the tribes went up, if not in full force, at least by their representatives, and the national *The prophet Azariah.* "The third month."

References and Authorities.

Baasha's attack.

Note C.

covenant was renewed with joy, "with shouting, and with trumpets, and with cornets."

Such demonstrations could not but be very highly offensive to Baasha; and his jealous anger may sufficiently account for the attack on Judah which soon followed, and which was described in the preceding section. The chronological difficulty is discussed in the Notes on the present chapter. There seems sufficient reason to conclude that the attack of the Israelite king upon Ramah, the alliance of Asa with Benhadad of Damascus, followed by the loss of Israelite territory north and south, and the renewed triumph of Judah, must be placed not long after the date of the Ethiopian invasion. Asa showed his politic skill in the positions selected for the fortresses which he erected from the spoils of Ramah. "Geba, which was situated opposite to Michmash, on the south side of a great ravine (1 Sam. xiv. 5), is almost certainly *Jeba*, which stands picturesquely on the top of its steep terraced hill, on the very edge of the great *Wady Suweinit*, looking northwards to the opposite village which retains its old name of Michmash" (*Porter*). "The position of Geba was thus exceedingly strong; and as it lay further north than Ramah, Asa may have considered that to fortify and garrison it would be a better protection to his northern frontier than fortifying Ramah." "Mizpah," too, "if situated on the northern continuation of the Mount of Olives, near the modern village of *Shafat*, would exactly cover Jerusalem in case of an invasion from the north. That it lay upon the direct road from Samaria is indicated by the history related in Jer. xli. 5—9; from which we also learn that Asa, besides fortifying the place, sank a deep well there to secure his garrison from want of water if the town should be besieged."

References and Authorities. Speaker's Comm. 1 Kings xiv. 22.

But again, in the very midst of these schemes and triumphs, a prophet appears upon the scene. Hanani the seer, perhaps father of that Jehu whom we have already seen as warning Baasha of approaching catastrophe, with stern faithfulness addressed king Asa. The burden of his reproof, as of so many prophets subsequently, was the alliance with a heathen power. After the great victory over Zerah, won in the name and by the might of the Lord, what but treasonable unfaithfulness was it to appeal to Benhadad against the inferior power of Baasha? It was a collapse of faith, sudden and sad. Prayer had been the king's sole resource when his army was confronted with the myriads of Ethiopia: was Israel mightier than Egypt? had prayer lost its efficacy, that worldly policy had become the king's only trust? Very significant are the prophet's words, "The king of Syria is escaped out of thine hand:" as much as to say, "The power of thy testimony as against heathenism and heathen nations is gone; the moral supremacy of Judah over idolatrous nations has been forfeited in this suppliant plea for their help." To such an appeal there could be but one reply. Asa could not refute the argument: he could at least imprison the prophet. Thus did he become a persecutor, to the manifest deterioration of his character. "He oppressed some of the people the same time." The prophet's reproof had applied a test under which he had

The prophet Hanani.

See p. 36.

Asa a persecutor.

References and Authorities. failed; and when arbitrary will had once triumphed over truth and reason, habits of tyranny were sure to follow.

Thus was Asa lost, but not wholly, in his self-sufficiency. His reign was still glorious, though tarnished. *Disease of the feet, generally thought to have been the gout.* At its close, bodily disease brought its humiliations, and as a proof of the self-sufficiency which had grown upon the monarch, we are told that "he sought not unto the Lord, but unto the physicians." It must be remembered, in explanation of this statement, that the recognised practitioners of medicine in Judea, as of all the liberal arts, were the Levites, who connected religious ceremonies and sanctions with all their practice, "calling," throughout, "upon the name of the Lord." The "physicians" were those who practised heathen arts of magic, disavowing recognised methods of cure, and dissociating the healing art from dependence on the God of Israel. The sin of Asa was not, therefore, in seeking medical advice, as we understand the phrase, but in forgetting Jehovah. The sacred historian evidently hints that the undue reliance on the "physi- *2 Chron. xvi. 12, literally, "in his disease also."* cians" was an illustration of the same weakness which had led Asa to rely upon the aid of Benhadad.

It would appear that the malady of the king proved fatal. After a reign—on the whole a very successful one—of forty-one years, he passed away, and the magnificence of his funeral ceremonies proved the *"A very great burning." Com- pare 2 Chron. xxi. 9. Jer. xxxiv. 5.* hold which he had established upon the regard of his subjects. It is significant that his son Jehoshaphat, a greater man perhaps in some respects than himself, began his reign by strengthening himself against Israel

For Judah was now distinctly devoted to the worship of Jehovah; Israel was becoming as distinctly idolatrous in the early days of Ahab and Jezebel. The two kingdoms were hereafter to contract an alliance fraught with evil, but the time had not yet come.

References and Authorities.

§ 3.—AHAB AND JEZEBEL.

In the long catalogue of royal transgressors the name of AHAB stands unenviably pre-eminent. "There was none like unto Ahab, which did sell himself to work wickedness in the sight of the Lord." Moral weakness was his undoing; and the main instigator of his evil deeds was Jezebel, his queen, daughter of Eth-baal, or Ithobal, king of Tyre and Sidon; a community sunk in degrading forms of idolatry. Eth-baal himself had been priest of Ashtoreth, but having murdered his brother, king Pheles, had usurped his throne. At the accession of Ahab Baal-worship was fast replacing the corrupt but less flagrant system of Jeroboam. The daughter of the Sidonian priest-king made her own goddess a special object of adoration; and the Phœnician deities, Baal and Ashtoreth, the male and female "abominations" of the surrounding heathen, were acknowledged as the patron gods of Israel. The prophets of Jehovah were persecuted, and many of them slain. We have no means of estimating the number who fell victims: the hundred preserved and nourished in secret by the king's steward, Obadiah, appear to have been but a remnant; from which it may be inferred that the teachers of the true faith

1 Kings xxi. 25.

See Josephus, *Ant.* viii. 12, 13.

Josephus, *cont. Apion* i. 18. Baal or *lord* (Moloch *king*), probably orig., the sun, Ashtoreth, or Astarte, the moon—symbol of the masculine and feminine principle respectively.

1 Kings xviii. 4; xix. 18.

50   *ISRAEL AND JUDAH,*

References and Authorities. had remained very numerous. Nor were they without adherents. Seven thousand men silently refused to the last to share in the national apostasy.

Rebuilding of Jericho. This record of the nation's departure from God almost engrosses the earlier annals of the reign, only one political incident being recorded, and that for the purpose of marking a divine judgment. The city of

BAAL AND ASHTORETH.

Josh. vi. 2. Jericho, smitten with utter destruction by Joshua more than six hundred years ago, had remained a ruin ever since, protected by an awful curse. Yet the situation must have attracted the longing eyes both of king and people. The " city of palm trees " in the valley of the Jordan was beautiful for situation, while a fortress commanding the access to the most practicable fords of the river would be invaluable for defence.

Whether any efforts had heretofore been made to traverse the divine decree we know not; we only read with appalling brevity how Hiel, an inhabitant of Bethel, attempted the task, and too fatally succeeded. As had been foretold, he "laid the foundation thereof in his firstborn, and set up the gates thereof in his youngest;" words by which we are undoubtedly to understand that at the commencement of the enterprise the former died, at its close the latter, as if smitten by the hand of God. The testimony to the certainty of divine warnings would be most impressive in that apostate age, proving Jehovah still to be the God of Israel, and showing that, though the prophets might be slain, the word of prophecy remained inviolably sure. Jericho remained, again to flourish in its pride to distant ages, and to welcome the passing presence of the Saviour of men; but its foundations and its towers would long be to all Israel a sign that "God is not mocked;" while the incident itself may have emboldened the prophet whose name is inseparably connected with the epoch to cross from his native Gilead—perhaps by those very fords—and to declare in solemn and majestic tones the counsels of the Most High. *[References and Authorities. Luke xix. 1.]*

ELIJAH was from a place unknown, Thisbe or Thesbon by name, among the Gileadite mountains. He bursts upon the scene with startling suddenness, clad in his hairy mantle, and proclaiming to king and people the approach of drought and famine. An apostle takes us into the secret of Elijah's power. *He had prayed* amid the solitudes of his Gileadite *[Elijah. James v. 17.]*

home; pleading with Jehovah His own cause in those days of national guilt, imploring some sign that might arouse the consciences of the people, fix their wavering decision, and even reach the royal heart. The sign was given, and the beneficent rains for three weary years were withheld from the parched land. The prophet who had foretold the visitation was directed to withdraw for a while from the scene of its greatest severity. First, he found a resting-place by the bed of a winter torrent rushing from the hills to the Jordan, where messengers—the unlikeliest to all human seeming—brought him daily food; then, when the stream was dry, in Zarephath (Sarepta), a city in the dominions of the very Eth-baal whose daughter sought the prophet's life—a retreat unlikelier still. Ahab, in impotent anger, inquired everywhere for the hiding-place of his stern reprover: probably the dominions of Jezebel's father were exempt from his search. Meanwhile Elijah was then as a peasant in the cottage of a poor widow, untraced and unsuspected. His presence brought plenty to that poverty-stricken family, and eventually life to the bed of death. Elijah, the stern witness against Phœnician idolatries, was himself the blessing of a Phœnician home. Profound and beautiful is the lesson of charity which he has thus left to mankind. Nor can we doubt that the heathen woman, so visited and blessed, learned to acknowledge Jehovah not only as the prophet's God, but as her own.

"Three years and six months" after the beginning of the famine,—"in the third year" of the prophet's

References and Authorities.

Cherith; it cannot now be identified. *Ravens*, or as some think *Arabians*, the roving inhabitants of the wilderness. See Kitto *Daily Bible Illust.* in loc.

1 Kings xviii. 10.

Luke iv. 25 26.

sojourn at Zarephath,—the time had fully come for his *References and Authorities.*
"showing unto Israel." The drought continued in its severity, as the records of heathen Tyre attest. Its dire consequences to man and beast we can but faintly conjecture; even the monarch was at length compelled to lay aside his state, and to travel in person through the land in quest of some forgotten cistern not yet dry, or deep springing well. The

MOUNT CARMEL.

incidents which led to the meeting of Ahab and Elijah are given in detail by the inspired narrator. It is plain from the king's first question to the prophet, "Art thou he that troubleth Israel?" that the thoughts of the former had throughout associated the calamity with the seer who first predicted it; and that, so far, the sign was understood.

References and Authorities.
The trial on Carmel.

The scene that followed—the trial on Mount Carmel—needs no description here. On some broad table-land of that wooded hill, with the purple sea to the west, the shrunken Kishon sweeping round the foot of the mountain, the sun-god of the Baal-worshippers glaring as if pitilessly on his votaries, the prophet of the Invisible One submits the question to a test. The people have gathered in their thousands from curiosity or from awe. They are still undecided,—in the prophet's figure like the bird which hops from bough to bough and will not rest on either. But they ostensibly prefer the stronger side, where the sullen king and his nobles, with the four hundred and fifty prophets of Baal and Ashtoreth, who have unwillingly come from Samaria to take their part in the great solemnity, are confronted by the man who is not ashamed to say before them all, "I, even I only, remain a prophet of the Lord." The invocations of the Baal-worshippers, with frantic outcries and self-inflicted wounds, show them to have been either strangely sincere in their belief, or perhaps only desperate. But their god still looks down with unpitying eye; and, blazing in the heavens, affords no spark to kindle the altar-fuel. At length they surrender the task in despair; then, with long preliminaries and solemn appeal to the Most High, Elijah, still solitary, prepares the sacrifice. The altar he constructs of *twelve* stones, not ten. In that supreme hour Elijah will not own a divided Kingdom. Israel is still ideally one, and Jehovah is God of all! The appeal is heard; the prophet's faith is honoured. The lightning falls from the cloudless heaven, the offering *References and Authorities.* is consumed, and the people, roused to sudden decision, cry aloud,* " JEHOVAH, He is the God: JEHOVAH, He is the God!"

And what are we to say of the human immolation that followed? Simply this—that the struggle was one for life or death. The prophets of the Lord and the priests of Baal could not live together in Israel. So long as they should co-exist side by side, so long would the people "halt between two opinions." It was needful at any cost to repress idolatry, and this was to be effected only by the destruction of the idol priests. The deed was a solemn, terrible *execution*, not a fanatical *massacre*—a warning to the impious king and queen, who had set themselves deliberately to violate the condition of the nation's existence. Idolatry was no mere religious error; it was treason, direct and defiant, against Israel's supreme King; and it was better that these four hundred and fifty priests should die than that the nation should become apostate and lost. The spirit of Christianity is different, in that the sphere of its action has passed from the outward and visible to the spiritual and unseen. Still do the ministers of Jehovah wield a sword, but it is "the sword of the Spirit;" and to the appeal of the zealot and the persecutor in every age, "shall we do *as Elijah did?*" the Master still *Luke ix. 54.*

Slaughter of Baal's prophets.

Deut. xiii. 5, 15, 16; xvii. 5.

---

* This is one of the passages in which the *name* of "Jehovah" (more correctly *Jahveh*) would convey the meaning better than the appellation, "Lord."

replies, "The Son of man is not come to destroy men's lives, but to save them."

Return of plenty.

After this great judicial act the nation, so to speak, breathed again freely. As though in sympathy with the restored life of Israel, nature resumed its course. The stifling drought was over; storm and refreshing shower proved anew the efficacy of Elijah's prayer. Very striking is the picture of Ahab in his chariot, impetuously urging his way to Jezreel (now first mentioned as a royal residence) to escape the force of the hurricane, while Elijah as an attendant runner speeds on before him. The great prophet was not above taking the position of Ahab's servant, and was as loyal as he was faithful to the king. Yet the first result of these great events was rather the exasperation of the court than the conversion of the people. This Elijah might have expected; but probably the confession of the thousands upon Carmel had made him too sanguine. At Jezreel he is no welcome guest. Instead of gathering the nation anew in fealty around the standard of Jehovah, he soon finds himself, to his own surprise and despair, a fugitive, solitary in the wilderness. His sorrowful depression and the divine manifestation which reassured his faith rank among the points of sublimest interest in the sacred story. The prophet is taught that God's mightiest working is in silence. His is the "still small voice" when storm and flame have passed; and so the terrors of Carmel did but prepare the way for a persuasive ministry, in which the power as well as the gentleness of His Spirit would be known.

Withdrawal of Elijah.

While thus, with new heart and hope, Elijah re-assumes his mission, consecrating Elisha as his assistant and successor, and renewing, as we shall see hereafter, his fearless appeal to king Ahab, great national disasters are impending over Israel. Benhadad, probably son of the old ally of Asa against Baasha, continued to harass the kingdom. In the time of Omri his father had compelled that king to allot him a portion in Samaria—a "Syrian quarter," as it would now be called,—"streets" exempt in some measure from Israelite jurisdiction. But not content with this, Benhadad now assaulted Samaria itself, with thirty-two "kings" or petty chieftains in his train. The haughty message which he sent to Ahab is quite Oriental in its tone. It was in vain that the king of Israel sought to stay his approach by a rejoinder of abject humility almost inexplicable. The demands of Benhadad only rise in insolence with Ahab's submissiveness; and it is good to see that even the weak spirit of the latter is aroused to refusal, and eventual defiance. Many who quote or hear the words, "Let not him that girdeth on his harness boast himself as he that putteth it off," have never thought to trace the proverbial saying to its source in the momentary nobleness of this most ignoble king. Nor was the revived courage of Ahab altogether fruitless. Once more a prophet of Jehovah presented himself before the king, but it was with words of happy augury. Another proof was to be given by the longsuffering God of Israel that only He was Lord.

Benhadad, in careless insolence, was carousing at the

References and Authorities.

Syrian invasion.

1 Kings xx. 34.

"Son of Hadad" probably, like *Pharaoh*, a general title.

Benhadad's insolence and defeat.

References and Authorities. gates of Samaria; and when word was brought that "men had come out of the city," he only issued the contemptuous order, "Take them alive!" But the spirit of the Israelites was aroused, and they fell upon the Syrians with irresistible force, putting them to flight, so that Benhadad himself fled in the confused rout. Ahab followed "the princes" by whom the onset had been made, and there was a great slaughter of the Syrians. With this victory the king seemed inclined to be content, but the prophet again appears, to rouse

Compare 1 Kings xi. 1. him from careless security. "At the return of the year"—the usual season for military operations—"the king of Syria will come up against thee." Whether a foreboding or an inspired prophecy, the word was fulfilled. Two reasons were assigned by the Syrians for their defeat. The first was the strong position of Ahab's capital. "The gods" of Israel "were gods of the hills:" the supernatural forces that protected Israel were imagined, in the Eastern pictorial way, as concentrated on the heights and pouring from the precipices of Samaria. It was not an unnatural supposition for those heathen to make. How many of the great events of Israelite history had been associated with mountains! Sinai and Hor and Pisgah, the "mountains round about Jerusalem," and more recently the wooded heights of Carmel, had attested Jehovah's presence and power. Canaan was a hill country; Syria was mostly a plain; perchance the Syrian deities might prove mightier on congenial ground, and in the open field "Syria would surely prevail over Israel." The second reason was sought

References and Authorities. in the inefficiency of the Syrian commanders. There were too many dignified personages among them,— too few true soldiers. "Take the kings away, and put *captains* in their room."

Aphek. Accordingly, at the season foreseen, the troops of Syria, marshalled and officered anew, appeared in "the Glen" at the head of the broad valley of Jezreel, and just below the Little Hermon. It was near to the field of more than one decisive battle. Gilboa bounded the horizon in the south, and Megiddo lay to the west: a battle of "Armageddon" was impending, which might have finally decided the supremacy of Israel over Syria. After a long pause the first blow was struck. The Israelite army, disposed apparently in two wings, and vividly pictured as like "two little flocks of kids" as against the vast array of Syrians that "filled the country," went up to battle in the strength of the Lord of hosts. The national conscience had been touched on Carmel; the national prowess revived at Aphek, and a hundred thousand Syrians fell on the battle plain. The remnant fled into the neighbouring city, which no doubt had been occupied by Benhadad on his march, but many

"A wall," ver. 30; perhaps 27,000 was the *whole* number escaped, some of whom were thus killed. *Kitto* supposes an earthquake.

were overwhelmed by the crash of a falling building. Benhadad, in his humiliation, was fain to seek refuge in an inner chamber. And now came the critical test of Ahab's character. The Syrian king and chieftains determined to throw themselves on his mercy; the king of Israel, forgetting that a righteous severity was the obligation of the hour, weakly gave way, as if alarmed by his own success. Most graphically is the wily Syrian embassage depicted. *References and Authorities.* The messengers of Benhadad came in humble suppliant guise, to "sound" Ahab as to his purpose with regard to the defeated king, and eagerly caught the word "brother" from his lips. They pressed their advantage, and Benhadad retired with the honours of war; the only humiliating condition imposed being that Israel should be permitted to occupy "streets" in Damascus. A sin was committed like the sin of *1 Sam. xv 22 23.* Saul in sparing Agag, and Ahab met with as stern a reproof. For new boldness now inspired the prophets *See ante, p. 57.* of Jehovah. In the trial on Carmel, in the cessation of famine, in the defeat of Syria, God had "pleaded His own cause," and the voice of His servants was once more heard in the land. By an expressive "acted parable" one of the younger prophets showed to Ahab the guilt incurred in sparing the heathen monarch. The king of Israel had no heart to resent the faithful reproof; but, cowering before the prophet's words, returned from his great victory in a mood strangely unlike that of a conqueror!—"heavy and displeased, to Samaria." The cloud in the north is broken, not dispersed; three years more, and the bolt will fall. A great private crime, meanwhile, displays yet further the unworthiness of the king, and deepens the lesson of the impending catastrophe.

The history of Naboth's vineyard is so fully and *Naboth's vineyard* graphically narrated by the inspired annalist that comment is almost superfluous. Jezreel, it seems, had succeeded to Tirzah as the favourite retreat of the Israelite royal family, and from its beauty and fertility was well worthy of the selection. It was "situated on the heights at the western extremity of Mount Gilboa, on the eastern borders of the Plain of Esdraelon, and about twenty-five miles north of Samaria. It was the Windsor of Israel. It is a fine site for a town, and commands a wide and noble view, overlooking on the west the whole of the great plain to the long ridge of Carmel, and extending in the opposite direction down the broad low valley to Beth-shean, and towards the mountains of Ajalon beyond the Jordan." The desire of Ahab to improve his property by the addition of Naboth's heritage, the sturdy refusal of the Israelite landowner to alienate his possession, and the king's unmanly repining, are all most vividly set before us. Naboth's refusal, it should be observed, was warranted not only by a yeoman's natural clinging to his ancestral soil, but by the direct command of God. His reply to Ahab, "Jehovah forbid it me!" was, in fact, an appeal to the divine law, however that law may have come to be disregarded. This no doubt added bitterness to Ahab's resentment, and helped to enkindle Jezebel's fury. In her words to her husband we catch the undertone of scorn:—"Dost thou now govern the kingdom of Israel?" "Do you call yourself *a king?*" "Leave all to me!" Her unscrupulous nature was equal to the occasion. Naboth perished through foul perjury. Ahab went down to take possession; but *Elijah was there before him!* History scarcely records a more dramatic scene. Instead of the vaunt of kingly triumph, we hear a cry almost as of despair! Once in proud indignation Ahab's demand had been, "Art

References and Authorities.

Kitto: *Daily Bible Illustrations*, in loc.

Lev. xxv. 23.
Num. xxxvi. 7.

thou he that troubleth Israel?" Now, in his words— "Hast thou found me, O mine enemy?"—there is not anger only, but alarm. For Elijah's bearing, like his message, was charged with doom. The house of Jeroboam had fallen; the house of Baasha had fallen; now should also the house of Omri fall! There, on the scene of Jezebel's foul crime, should she miserably perish! And there also should the dogs lick up the blood of Ahab! Elijah had declared God's judgment —he was gone! Ahab returned in his wretchedness to his palace, a very genuine mourner now. Part of the doom is even postponed. For, as the history shows, it was not the blood of Ahab himself, but of Jehoram, his godless son, that stained the ground of Naboth's vineyard in Jezreel. *References and Authorities. 1 Kings xviii. 17. Comp. 1 Kings xxii. 38. 2 Kings ix. 24—26.*

Soon after these events, the annals of Israel and Judah become once more intermingled, but not for mutual good. Already had JEHOSHAPHAT, the godly and patriotic prince of the house of David, committed one terrible mistake in permitting the marriage of his son Jehoram with Athaliah, the daughter of Ahab and Jezebel. This alliance brought the monarchs into close intercourse, and three years after the great victory of Israel over Syria we find Jehoshaphat in Samaria. Ahab, as if dissatisfied with the terms of his compact with Benhadad, is seeking to break that inauspicious alliance. Occasion is found in the continued occupancy of Ramoth-gilead by the Syrians, contrary to the express stipulation with Benhadad; and Ahab wins from Jehoshaphat too ready a consent to join in an effort for its recapture. The transaction *Alliance with Jehoshaphat. 2 Kings viii. 18. 2 Chron. xviii. 1. Ramoth-Gilead. See 1 Kings xx. 34.*

is memorable, not only as leading to Ahab's death, but as exhibiting the "prophets" of Israel in a new and unfavourable light. The class had become professional; and though the name of Baal, since that memorable day on Carmel, was no longer great in Israel, there was no true allegiance to Jehovah on the part of these teachers of the people. Their aim was to flatter the king rather than to declare the truth. Four hundred at once were gathered at Ahab's command, and promised him victory at Ramoth-gilead, evading (it is observable) the use of the name Jehovah so long as they dared. It was not until Jehoshaphat had openly expressed his distrust of their words that one of them, Zedekiah, profaned that name by associating it with his false prophecy. The reluctance of Ahab to send for Micaiah—that prophet of inconvenient honesty!—was in perfect conformity with the king's character. Elijah was not to be *sent for*: it was his function to appear as the Lord his God might commission him. But at Jehoshaphat's urgent instance Micaiah came. In most impressive imagery he declared the approaching fall of Ahab; but not even thus were the kings deterred from the expedition. "The king of Israel disguised himself"—cowardly to the last; leaving Jehoshaphat to wear the royal panoply, which would be a sure mark for the enemy. But the device failed, as it deserved to fail: Benhadad sought only the life of Ahab. Jehoshaphat in his peril "cried out" in prayer to God, and God interfered to save him. The king of Syria had given instructions to all his captains to aim at the life of the

References and Authorities.

1 Kings xxii. 6. "The Lord" (Adonai) 2 Chron. xviii. 5 "God" (Elohim).

Micaiah now first mentioned by name (see xx. 35).

"A lying spirit."

king of Israel; but, as if to show the futility of human plans, it was not through this deep-laid scheme that Ahab fell, but through the "simplicity" of a certain man who "drew his bow at a venture." To the end, Ahab concealed his hurt as well as he was able; he was physically brave though morally so weak; but at sunset he expired, and the armies dispersed with their end unaccomplished, while Jehoshaphat returned home in peace, thankful to escape, and not unmindful of the lesson which, as we shall see, he also was to receive from an aged prophet's lips.

References and Authorities.
Heb. (margin)
Death of Ahab.

§ 4.—Jehoshaphat, King of Judah.

Before passing to the inglorious history of Ahab's successors on the throne of Israel, we may note the contrast which the southern kingdom presented, in the character and career of JEHOSHAPHAT, son of the almost equally illustrious Asa.

Ascending the throne at the age of thirty-five, Jehoshaphat followed in his father's footsteps, taking their greater ancestor David as his model. Ahab had already occupied the throne of Israel for some three years, but the king of Judah deliberately repudiated his evil courses. Happy, had he also declined that "affinity" which was the one blemish of Jehoshaphat's reign! Like his predecessors, he strengthened the borders of his land and garrisoned the frontier fortresses, obtaining also, without oppression, a liberal revenue from the people; and so administering the national affairs that surrounding nations, anxious for

Jehoshaphat's first measures.
"Sought not unto Baalim."
"Not after the doings of Israel."
"All Judah gave presents."

the alliance of Judah, offered a voluntary tribute. But it was not even in these respects that Jehoshaphat's wisdom showed most brightly. For to him, perhaps, first among the kings of Judah, belongs the imperishable honour of having instituted a system of national instruction. The names of his first teachers are recorded. Five were "princes," two were priests, nine were Levites; and with the authority of a royal commission, these sixteen men "taught in Judah, and had the book of the law of the Lord with them, and went about throughout all the cities of Judah, and taught the people." This little army of instructors, with the divine oracles in their hands, surely wrought a nobler work for Judah than even "the mighty men of valour that were in Jerusalem."

It is sad to have to turn, after these records of wise administration, successful commerce, and efforts for the people's good, to the history of the alliance between the servant of Jehovah and the votary of Baal, with their joint expedition to Ramoth-gilead. This was about the seventeenth year of Jehoshaphat's reign. Returning from the scene of Ahab's death, the king of Judah encountered the aged prophet Jehu, who rebuked him for the unequal alliance; the king, unlike Asa on a similar occasion, receiving the reproof in submissive silence. Hereafter the annals of Jehoshaphat are, with two notable exceptions, a record of the continuance of his wise endeavours to instruct the people, as well as of his earnest care to cover the land with just and impartial tribunals. It is observable that in these courts the secular and the spiritual functions were associated though distinct, a copartnery being instituted between Amariah, the chief priest in all matters of the Lord, and Zebadiah the son of Ishmael, the "ruler of the house of Israel for all the king's matters." In all this the king seems to be striving to act up to the spirit of his own name "Jehovah is Judge."

References and Authorities.

But now in the full tide of prosperity an unexpected invasion from the East brings a sudden panic upon the realm. "The children of Moab, and the children of Ammon, and the inhabitants of Mount Seir," with probably other tribes, combine against Judah, and are announced as approaching from the south along the valleys to the west of the Dead Sea. The danger seemed serious, especially as the armies of Judah were not on a warlike footing. It is difficult to resist the impression that the 83rd Psalm refers to this invasion :—

Invasion of Eastern hordes.

Psalm, lxxxiii., by "Asaph."

> "They have consulted together with one consent;
> They are confederate against Thee:
> The tabernacles of Edom, and the Ishmaelites,
> Of Moab, and the Hagarenes;
> Gebal, and Ammon, and Amalek;
> The Philistines with the inhabitants of Tyre.
> Assur also is joined with them:
> They have holpen the children of Lot."

The crisis is met, not by military preparations, but by fasting and prayer. Never was appeal to the Lord of hosts more touching in its fervent simplicity,—"O our God, wilt Thou not judge them? for we have no might against this great company that cometh against us; neither know we what to do; but our eyes are upon Thee." The appeal was heard. The Spirit of

The "Hallelujah victory."

References and Authorities. the Lord came upon a Levite of the sons of Asaph—perhaps the author of the Psalm already quoted—and from his lips rang forth the thrilling summons, fraught with memories of the Red Sea shores,—

Exod. xiv. 13. "STAND STILL AND SEE THE SALVATION OF JEHOVAH."

The inspired narrator records the wonders of the day that followed. At the head of Jehoshaphat's army marched the singers of the temple. Face to face with the enemy, they raised the loud HALLELUJAH—" Praise the Lord, for His mercy endureth for ever!" Then, as if smitten by some wild impulse, the confederate hosts turn their arms one against another. Ammon and Moab fall upon Mount Seir, and when the work of destruction is over they engage in mutual destructive fray. Judah looks on in trembling amazement, then advances to gather the mighty spoil. In this and in the burial of the dead three days are passed; and on the fourth day the rejoicing people gather for a solemn

The Kings Dale," act of praise in a valley near the scene of these marvels
Gen. xiv. 17. —a place henceforth to be known as the "Valley of Jehoshaphat," otherwise BERACHAH, or "Blessing;" for there the nation set the seal of its Amen upon the Hallelujah which had gotten them the victory.

Failure of maritime enterprise. The second great incident which marked the close of Jehoshaphat's reign, the campaign against Moab, rather belongs to the history of the northern kingdom, and will be considered in the next section. It seems surprising that the two kingdoms should again form military alliance after the bitter experience of Ramoth-gilead; but repeated warnings were needed; and a brief intimation in the history shows

TO THE CLOSE OF OMRI'S DYNASTY. 69

that although in one instance the joint forces of Jehosha- *References and Authorities.*
phat and the son of Ahab won a signal victory, it was
only to be followed by a yet more signal misfortune.
The tale is briefly told in these words, that "Jehoshaphat joined himself with Ahaziah to make ships to go
to Tarshish, and they made the ships in Ezion-geber." *Or, "to go to Ophir for gold."*
A prophet, one Eliezer, protested against the enter-
prise, predicting shipwreck: "Because thou hast joined
thyself with Ahaziah, the Lord hath broken thy works."
The words were brought to pass. "The ships were
broken at Ezion-geber," wrecked in port,—a great commercial disaster, dimly shadowed to us, but calculated
to cast a deep depression over the close of this great
and noble reign. At the age of sixty Jehoshaphat *Death of Jehoshaphat*
passed away, leaving as heir to his crown a son
unworthy of such parentage, the husband of the fierce
and cruel Athaliah.

§ 5.—THE TWO KINGDOMS UNTIL JEHU.

After the death of Ahab, two of his sons in suc-
cession occupied the throne of Israel. First AHAZIAH *Ahaziah. Compare*
reigned for little more than a year, dying through the *1 Kings xxi. 51.*
effect of a fall from his palace window. *2 Kings iii. 1.*

In connection with this fatality we have to note the *Reappearance of*
final appearance of the prophet Elijah before his *Elijah.*
translation. The king was sending messengers to the
Philistian oracle of Baal-zebub, "the lord of flies,"
at Ekron. The prophet of Jehovah met them on
their way, sternly denounced their errand to the idol
shrine, and bade them return to their master with
the forewarning of his speedy death. The king, in a

References and Authorities. fury, sent detachments of soldiers to apprehend Elijah, who called down fire from heaven to destroy them. Thus did he show how vain was the force of man against the majesty of God. But when the display of violence was exchanged for submissive entreaty, the prophet no more evoked the terror of the Lord, but came willingly to the royal bedside. There he could but repeat the message which he had received from God, and soon afterwards Ahaziah died.

Jehoram. He was succeeded by his brother, JEHORAM, or JORAM, who held the throne for twelve years. In his reign the reaction from Baal-worship, which dates from the trial on Carmel, seems to have been complete. Although Jezebel was still living, her son repudiated her special idolatry, and, perhaps as a compromise, reverted to the earlier system of Jeroboam. It was possibly because Jehoram professed himself a worshipper of Jehovah, although in this corrupt form, that Jehoshaphat showed himself willing to re-enter into alliance with Israel.

Translation of Elijah. One great event, all but unique in the history of mankind, marked the opening of Jehoram's reign. The prophet Elijah, the solitary witness for God in the darkest hour of Israelite history, had now closed his testimony, and was to receive one crowning token of the divine approval. The narrative in the second chapter of the Second Book of Kings shows to us "a great mystery;" Elisha only was permitted to view the outward symbols of the event—the "chariot of fire and horses of fire" being but emblems of that wondrous transformation by which "in a moment, in the twinkling of an eye," "the mortal put on immortality." The sons of the prophets, who had stood to view afar off, gave their testimony to the great prophet's disappearance; and the translation of Elijah, like that of Enoch in the days before the flood, gave to an unbelieving world a glimpse of that "life and incorruption" which a greater One was to "bring to light." References and Authorities. Gen. v. 24. Heb. xi. 5.

Elijah had been to Israel as a second Moses. The elder prophet declared God's law, his great follower restored it. The one delivered Israel from the idolatry of Egypt, the other saved the ten tribes from the Baal-worship of Phœnicia. Both wrought miracles, now of judgment, now of mercy. "Horeb, the mount of God," was to both the scene of highest inspiration; and in the manner and period of their fasting the resemblance was complete. The method of their departure from life, though different in each case, was alike significant. To Moses, amid the crags of Nebo, death had lost its sting; to Elijah, in the vale of the Jordan, the grave was despoiled of its victory. They were God's "two witnesses;" Law and Prophecy severally impersonated; often "cast out" by men, but destined to "rise and stand upon their feet" in living power. And still their highest, noblest testimony to the world is when they bring their tribute to "the man Christ Jesus," and speak with Him of "the decease" to be "accomplished at Jerusalem." Moses and Elijah. See Deut. xxxiv. Rev. xi. 3—12. Luke ix. 31.

To Moses had succeeded Joshua: after Elijah came Elisha; the departing prophet's falling mantle resting

References and Authorities. on and designating his successor in the great work of national reformation. By "a double portion" of Elijah's spirit must not be understood an actual superiority in endowments or power: the phrase is an allusion to the law of inheritance; the firstborn, as chief heir, having a double share of the family property. In this case the heritage was the honour and responsibility of the prophetic task; and this Elisha now set himself to discharge, not, as Elijah, dwelling apart, and appearing ever and anon at a crisis, but taking up his abode amongst men, and acting as the trusted counsellor of the king.

Elisha. It was in connection with the new alliance between Israel and Judah that the prophetic greatness of Elisha first conspicuously appears. The power of Moab had long been threatening the kingdom. No sooner had Ahab died than the Moabite chieftain *Sam. viii. 2* Mesha abjured the fealty to which the nation had been held since the days of David. Refusing, in the reign of Ahaziah, to continue their stipulated tribute, *"An hundred thousand lambs and an hundred thousand rams, with the wool."* they had been left awhile to "rebel" with impunity; but Jehoram, with the alliance of Jehoshaphat, as well as that of his vassal king of Edom, now felt himself strong enough to exact the old allegiance. The joint army found itself without water in the wilderness of Edom, and called in the emergency for a prophet of Jehovah. The name of Elisha was mentioned; and the three kings sought an audience with the prophet. His first words were reproachful, almost ungracious, intended no doubt as a test of Jehoram's real belief. "Get thee to the prophets of thy father, and to the prophets of thy mother." Jehoram answered humbly, *References and Authorities.* declaring himself, by implication, to be an adherent of Jehovah. But Elisha still regards him sternly, and consents to invoke the divine oracle only because of the presence of Jehoshaphat. His next words are remarkable,—*Bring a minstrel!*— as though he "needed first to calm down the perturbations of his spirit, to bring his soul into a fit form for receiving the intimations he sought from heaven, and to bear his spirit upon the wings of melodious sounds into the harmonious company around that throne which no dissonance can approach." The heavenly impulse came; the prophet ordered that the arid plain should be filled with ditches to receive the longed-for flood. *Kitto. Daily Scripture Illustrations.*

Scarcely was this accomplished when the torrent came and inundated the country. The armies were delivered from the tortures of thirst; nor only so, but when the sunrise gleamed redly on the pools, the Moabites, who had early donned their battle array, mistook the appearance for that of blood, and, suspecting that the Edomites had risen treacherously against Israel and put the armies of Jehoram and Jehoshaphat to the sword, dashed madly forward to share the spoil. It was a fatal mistake. The three kings were ready to receive the onset; the Moabites, already in confusion, were hopelessly routed, and their land occupied by the victorious Hebrew and Edomite forces. The Moabite king retired to Kir-haraseth, his strongest fortress, which was soon invested by the three kings. Baffled in an attempt to force his way out through the Edomite forces, king

74   ISRAEL AND JUDAH,

References and Authorities. Mesha retired to his city, and offered upon the wall his own son as a burnt sacrifice. The Israelites, horror-stricken, raised the siege and departed, but from that time Moab was so weakened, that we no more meet with it in history as an aggressive power. Only a later prophet announces its final and complete destruction. The history of the nation has in recent times acquired new interest from the discovery of the "Moabite stone," a monument belonging to the time of King Mesha.

Isaiah xv., xvi. (See Note C, p. 88.)

Jehoram. On the death of Jehoshaphat, which occurred soon after these events, his son JEHORAM, the husband of Ahab's daughter Athaliah, succeeded to the throne in Jerusalem, having been associated with his father in the government for some years previously. Two kings of the same name were thus for a short time contemporary in the two kingdoms, a fact which to some readers of Scripture is a little perplexing, especially since the predecessor and brother of the Israelite Jehoram, and the successor and son of the Judæan Jehoram, bore the same name, Ahaziah. A glance at the table prefixed to the present chapter will make this sufficiently plain.

Two Jehorams. Two Ahaziahs.

The son of Jehoshaphat

It is mournful to see that of the two Jehorams the son of Jehoshaphat was pre-eminent in wickedness. So soon as he attained the sole sovereignty he put his brothers to death, involving in the massacre several of the chief men of Judah. To this crime he added the practice of an idolatry even fouler than that of the northern kingdom. Only the faithfulness of God to His covenant withheld the merited doom from falling upon king and people together. The relapse into heathen wickedness was the worst that Judah yet had known. A prophetic writing of Elijah the prophet, left by him before his translation, as a "letter to the king of Judah," was discovered and given in vain to the apostate king. As the nation departed from God its power became enfeebled. First, the Edomites, whom we have seen associated with Judah and Israel in the attack on Moab, revolted from the Hebrew yoke, Jehoram putting forth his power to crush the rebellion in vain. The Philistines also, and the hordes of the Arabian desert, emboldened by the feebleness of Judah, penetrated in their incursions as far as Jerusalem, even carrying away the wives and striking down the sons of the king,—only Ahaziah, youngest of the princes, the future king, being left alive.

References and Authorities.
Letter from Elijah, his only writing.

Or Jehoahas. 2 Chron. xxi. 17. or Azariah, xxii. 6.

While Judah was thus sinking deeper into degradation its sister kingdom was engaged in a long struggle with Syria. Elisha was still the trusted counsellor of his sovereign. The cure of Naaman, the Syrian general, showed that in the intermission of hostilities some friendly relations subsisted between the two courts, although at best the agreement was that of an "armed truce." At the siege of Dothan a direct though abortive effort was made by the troops of Benhadad to capture the prophet, while the investment of Samaria by the Syrian forces a little later was followed by one of the most signal deliverances ever wrought for Israel. At length, when the mighty Benhadad was upon his death-bed, he condescended to inquire concerning the result of his illness from the

Israel and Syria.

prophet whom he had so often treated as an enemy. The king's emissary was Hazael, whose designs upon the Syrian throne Elisha well knew. The subtle diplomatist had his inmost thoughts unveiled by the fearless prophet, and returned at once to deceive and to slay the royal master who had trusted him. Benhadad died, and Hazael, according to prophetic announcement made long before, became the king of Syria.

References and Authorities.
See Note D, p. 89.

Now again did the monarchs of the two Hebrew kingdoms enter into a disastrous alliance. Jehoram of Judah was dead,—smitten by a painful and loathsome disease, and departing unlamented. He "departed without being desired." His youngest son, Ahaziah, had succeeded him, at the age of twenty-two. Jehoram of Israel had resolved to make another attempt upon Ramoth-gilead, and solicited the assistance of his sister's son. Ahaziah obeyed the summons, and once again the forces of Israel and Judah were joined before the ill-omened city. As if to carry the parallel farther, the king of Israel was wounded in Ramoth by the Syrians, and this also led to his final undoing. Compelled by his wound to quit the scene of warfare, he had retired to Jezreel for cure, leaving the command to his general, Jehu. Ahaziah, king of Judah, had also gone to visit his uncle; and the two kings were together at the summer palace of the latter, unaware of any intended harm.

New alliances: Judah and Israel.

Not 42, as 2 Chron. xxii. 2. See 2 Kings viii. 26.

Called also Ramah.

Suddenly in the camp at Ramoth there appeared a son of the prophets, an emissary of Elisha, who, calling Jehu from the company of officers, anointed him king over Israel, declaring that by him should be

Jehu anointed King.

accomplished the predicted doom of Ahab's house, *References and Authorities.* on which "he opened the door and fled." Jehu returned in great excitement to the mess table; the errand of the prophet was soon elicited, when the officers, with one accord, threw off their allegiance to Jehoram, and with joyful acclamations saluted Jehu as king. He, on his part, enjoined secrecy for the moment; none but he must bear the news of deposition to Jehoram. The sequel is narrated with wonderful vividness. The swift chariot ride of Jehu with his company from Ramoth to Jezreel, his reception of the several messengers sent to inquire his errand, the final egress of the kings to meet him, the encounter of Jehoram and Jehu on the plot of ground where Naboth's vineyard had been, and the assassination of the two kings, form the successive scenes of the revolution, swift and terrible; the events of a single day at a stroke depriving two kingdoms of their rulers, changing the destinies of Israel, and even threatening the house of David with extinction. But all was not yet over. The real instigator of the idolatries of Israel was yet to be reached. Jehoram was comparatively guiltless, the sin lay chiefly at the door of Jezebel. Jehu accordingly pursued his way to Jezreel. The queen-mother was prepared to meet him, though by this time conscious that the hour of her doom had come. With some dignity she prepared herself as for a visit of state—for the painting of her eyes and the adjustment of her head-dress *See margin 1 Kings ix. 30* were but the customary toilet of royal or noble ladies; and, instead of shrinking into retirement, she

References and Authorities. boldly addressed to Jehu on his approach the stinging words, "Had Zimri peace who slew his master?" The only reply of the fierce soldier was to bid that she be flung down forthwith; and without staying to heed her prostrate form, he drove over her body to the palace. The wild dogs of the city consumed her unhonoured remains—terrible fulfilment of Elijah's word to Ahab, "The dogs shall eat Jezebel by the wall [or ditch] of Jezreel."

So fell Ahab's house; but the fierce purpose of Jehu was not yet accomplished. Perhaps there is no more terrible chapter in the whole of Scripture than the tenth in the Second Book of Kings, in its record of unsparing bloodshed. The plea for Jehu must be that he thought himself to be the instrument of a divine purpose. In truth, he *had* a commission, although he carried it unwarrantably far. His "zeal" was for the "Lord of hosts;" but in the end he seems to have mistaken the instinct of bloodthirstiness for the dictate of religion. The chapter records a threefold massacre. First, the "seventy sons of Ahab," including, it may be, nephews and grandchildren, several of whom would be of tender years, who had been entrusted for nurture to the chief men of Samaria, were slain by them at Jehu's command. Then forty-two, relatives of Ahaziah, on their way to join the royal party at Samaria, in ignorance of what had happened, were arrested and remorselessly put to death. And lastly, the few remaining worshippers of Baal were decoyed by an inexcusable stratagem into the temple of that false deity, where they were seized and slain, the images

Threefold immolation.

Ahab's descendants.

Ahaziah's relatives.

Baal-worshippers.

being broken and the temple defiled. Throughout these transactions Jehu appears the same—determined, unscrupulous, self-complacent, also with a strange grim humour, as when he sent to the elders of Samaria, proposing that they should elect a king out of Ahab's seventy sons, and afterwards when, as the heads of these hapless youths were heaped up by his orders at the city gates, he said to the elders, " Ye be righteous; behold, *I* conspired against my master and slew him; but *who slew all these?*" The best that can be said of him was that he accomplished the predestined doom of a guilty house; but his own heart was not right with God. *[References and Authorities. Character of Jehu.]*

After these sanguinary deeds, none were left to resist the claim of Jehu to the throne of Israel. In Jerusalem the situation was more critical; and the queen-mother, Athaliah, true daughter of Jezebel, with unnatural cruelty, destroyed her own grandchildren, that she might usurp the throne. But for the wonderful providence of God, the "lamp" of David's house would have been extinguished in that dark hour. *[The two kingdoms. Athaliah.]*

§ 6.—ELISHA.

Before passing to the next stage of the history, it may be useful to revert to the career of the extraordinary man who, all through the reign of Jehoram, and in a measure also through the three following, had so great a share in influencing the policy of the Israelitish kingdom. ELISHA was in truth what upon his death-bed he was declared to be by royal lips, "the chariot of Israel, and the horsemen thereof." *[2 Kings xiii. 14. Elisha's own words to the departing Elijah, ii. 12.]*

The difference between Elijah and his successor

References and Authorities. must strike every reader. The older and the greater prophet for the most part lived in retirement; appearing suddenly and on great occasions, and for the most part delivering an unregarded testimony to "a stiffnecked and rebellious people." His miracles were comparatively few, but stupendous. His prayers opened and closed the heavens; he invoked celestial fire to consume the sacrifice on Carmel; and from "the top of a hill," called down the lightning to destroy those who would take him captive. Elisha wrought many miracles, but mostly of a homelier character. Those recorded in Scripture are the following:

2 Kings ii. 14	The Jordan divided (so Elijah).
ii. 21, 22.	The waters healed.
iv. 1—7.	The widow's oil multiplied (so Elijah).
iv. 32—37.	The Shunammite's child restored (so Elijah at Zarephath).
iv. 39—41.	Poisonous pottage rendered wholesome.
iv. 42—44.	Food miraculously multiplied.
v. 13, 14.	Naaman cured of leprosy.
vi. 6.	The iron axe head made to swim.
vi. 18.	Syrians smitten with blindness.

May we add the miracle wrought even by his bones in the sepulchre, on touching which a dead man "revived and stood up upon his feet"? Some of these wonders, as may be seen, are almost exactly paralleled in Elijah's history; but for the most part they belong to the ordinary life which the later prophet spent among his own order at Bethel, Gilgal, and Jericho, where the "schools of the prophets" were situated. The exercise of these gifts marked him out as a man specially favoured by God, and appointed at a critical time to guide the destinies of Israel.

To this end also the divine judgment upon the mocking youths at Bethel evidently contributed. That forty and two "little children" should have been torn by she-bears for the offence of scoffing at a prophet seems at first sight very terrible. But a little closer examination will shed new light upon the matter. In the first place the mockers were not necessarily *children.* The term used of those who were torn by the bears" is applied to Ishmael when he was about fourteen years old ; to Isaac when he was grown up to be a young man; to Shechem the son of Hamor when of marriageable age, and probably not less than twenty years old ; to Joseph when he was seventeen; to Gideon's son, Jether, when old enough to be ordered to slay two kings ; to Solomon after he had become king; to the four hundred Amalekites who escaped on camels; to Elisha's servant Gehazi; to the sons of the prophets who anointed Jehu; to the two hundred and thirty-two attendants of the princes of the provinces who went out against Benhadad; to the soldiers of the Assyrian king ; and in other places too numerous to cite. In all these cases, though differently translated, according to the apparent meaning of the sacred writer, by *child, lad, young man, servant,* the word is but one in the original, and is the same which is here employed to express '*children.*'" Again, the words "*Go up*" were not a mere expression of juvenile ridicule; they seem to refer very plainly to the translation of Elijah, who

References and Authorities.

2 Kings ii. 23—25.

Na'ar.
Gen xxi. 16.
Gen. xxii. 12.
Gen. xxxiv. 19.
Gen. xxxvii. 2.
Judges viii. 20.
1 Kings iii. 7.
1 Sam. xxx. 17.
2 Kings iv. 12.
2 Kings ix. 4.
1 Kings xx. 15.
2 Kings xix. 6.

Kitto: *Daily Bible Illustrations.*

G

had "gone up" as by a chariot of fire into heaven. The phrase is a taunt, expressing contemptuous disbelief—"*Ascend! as thou sayest thy master has done!*" It was an insult not only to the prophets but to their Lord—a *deliberate* insult, for these lads "came forth out of the city" to offer it.* The punishment that overtook them was therefore the doom of wanton and insolent unbelief; a proof added to the many that were needed in that sceptical age that there was indeed a God in Israel.

The part which Elisha took in the anointing of two kings, Hazael and Jehu, has already been noted. In both cases the prophet declared the secrets of futurity as made known to him by the Most High; but in neither was he responsible for the method by which the event was brought to pass. Hazael and Jehu alike wrought their ends by murder, but for all this their evil deeds were overruled by God for His own purposes. The elevation of Hazael had even been predicted to Elijah, in connection with the destruction of the Baal-worship in Israel; and, as a matter of fact, the Syrian invasions which followed the death of Benhadad led, however indirectly, to the extirpation of this foul idolatry.

It only remains to notice the very striking conference between the prophet and Naaman, the Syrian general. Several points in the narrative need no comment, as the pride of Naaman—the lesson of humility needed

---

* *Bald-head* could scarcely have referred to Elisha's great age, as he lived more than fifty years afterwards. Probably it denoted some arrangement of the hair that showed him to be a prophet.

by him before he could be healed—the disinterested-ness of Elisha—the falsehood of Gehazi and its detection. The whole transaction is remarkable, as an instance of *religious* connection between Syria and Israel. The idol-worshipper was not only constrained to seek for healing from the prophet of Jehovah, but confessed the God of Israel as supreme. But what followed? A superstitious request, and an appeal for toleration. To these the prophet answered, "Go in peace"—no mere conventional farewell, as we understand the words, for to withhold all reply to Naaman's request would surely have been uncourteous. Rather may we see in Elisha's language the kindly tolerance of an imperfect faith. Let Naaman take of the soil of Palestine if he will: there can be no intrinsic superiority in an altar of such material; but should the association lift the worshipper's mind to higher things, so let it be. Imperfect faith may need a help, which to a manlier or more mature religion would be only a superstition. Then, even if Naaman should outwardly bow before Rimmon while his spirit is erect and free—forced to the external act, as he persuades himself, by the pressure of circumstances,—he is to be pitied in his self-delusion rather than sternly condemned. If he is sincere he will be sure to learn not to palter with his conviction. Already he feels the need of forgiveness for the act: "The Lord pardon thy servant in this thing." He may safely be left to his own conscience to teach him in the end a higher truth; and the prophet's large-hearted tolerance of the remaining weaknesses in the faith of his convert is not the

References and Authorities.
Ver. 16. com
ch. viii. 8. 9.
Ver. 20—27.

Ver. 17—19.

Comp. "the water of Jordan" for baptisms: bread from Bethlehem for the Lord's Supper, &c.

least noteworthy part of his witness for the God of Israel.

After the accession of Jehu we read no more of Elisha for about five-and-forty years. The prophet could not but mourn over the character of those who now held sway in Israel; the vigour of his own life was passed; the day of miracle was over; his work was almost done. One flash of the old prophetic spirit appears upon his death-bed; then, full of years and honours, he passed away.

NOTES ON CHAPTER III.
A.—THE PARALLEL HISTORIES.

In the present section the divergence of the two histories becomes remarkable. The Books of Chronicles are almost wholly occupied by the kingdom of Judah; the Books of Kings have chiefly to do with Israel and its two great prophets. Elijah is mentioned only once in the Chronicles after his death; Elisha not at all. In the following list the passages are classified.

I. NARRATIVES COMMON TO THE TWO.

Accession and Piety of Asa, 1 Kings xv. 9—15; 2 Chron. xiv. 1—5; evidently two independent accounts.

Invasion of Judah by Baasha, 1 Kings xv. 16—22; 2 Chron. xvi. 1—6; the same account substantially. The former adds Cinneroth (Gennesaret) to the districts overrun by the Israelites. The reproof by Hanani the seer is added in the Chronicles only, ver. 7—10.

Death of Asa, 1 Kings xv. 23, 24; 2 Chron. xvi. 11—14. The passages are subjoined; observe the additions in the Chronicles :—

1 Kings xv. 23, 24.

"The rest of all the acts of Asa, and all his might, and all that he did, and the cities which he built, are they not written in the book of the chronicles of the kings of Judah? Nevertheless in the time of his old age he was diseased in his feet. And Asa slept with his fathers, and was buried with his fathers in the city of David his father : and Jehoshaphat his son reigned in his stead."

2 Chron. xvi. 11—14.

"And, behold, the acts of Asa, first and last, lo, they are written in the book of the kings of Judah and Israel. And Asa in the thirty and ninth year of his reign was diseased in his feet, until his disease was exceeding great : yet in his disease he sought not to the Lord, but to the physicians. And Asa slept with his fathers, and died in the one and fortieth year of his reign. And they buried him in his own sepulchres, which he had made himself in the city of David, and laid him in the bed which was filled with sweet odours and divers kind of spices prepared by the apothecaries' art : and they made a very great burning for him."

Accession of Jehoshaphat, 1 Kings xv. 24; xxii. 41—46 ; 2 Chron. xvii. 1—6.

Shipwreck of Jehoshaphat's fleet, 1 Kings xxii. 48, 49 ; 2 Chron. xx. 35—37. These two remarkable passages are subjoined. It is evident that the refusal mentioned in Kings belongs to a *second* application.

1 Kings xxii. 49.

"Jehoshaphat made ships of Tharshish to go to Ophir for gold : but they went not; for the ships were broken at Ezion-geber. Then said Ahaziah the son of Ahab unto Jehoshaphat, Let my servants go with thy servants in the ships. But Jehoshaphat would not."

2 Chron. xx. 35—37.

"And after this did Jehoshaphat, king of Judah, join himself with Ahaziah, king of Israel, who did very wickedly : and he joined himself with him to make ships to go to Tarshish : and they made the ships in Ezion-gaber. Then Eliezer, the son of Dodavah, of Mareshah, prophesied against Jehoshaphat, saying, Because thou hast joined thyself with Ahaziah, the Lord hath broken thy works. And the ships were broken, that they were not able to go to Tarshish."

Joint expedition of Ahab and Jehoshaphat to Ramoth-gilead, 1 Kings xxii. 1—36; 2 Chron. xviii. 1—34; evidently the same account.

Accession and reign of Jehoram, son of Jehoshaphat; Revolt of Edom from Judah, 2 Kings viii. 16—22; 2 Chron. xxi. 5—10; plainly the same paragraph, except that the Chronicler gives the reason of Jehoram's disasters—"because he had forsaken the Lord God of his fathers."

Accession of Ahaziah, king of Judah, 2 Kings ix. 25—27; 2 Chron. xxii. 1—4; two independent accounts.

Joint expedition of Ahaziah and Jehoram to Ramoth-gilead.—Visit by the former to the latter at Jezreel, 2 Kings viii. 28, 29; 1 Chron. xxii. 5—9. The Chronicler adds a brief account of the death of the two kings, which the earlier historian gives in detail.

II. NARRATIVES PECULIAR TO THE BOOKS OF KINGS.

The doom pronounced on Baasha and his house, 1 Kings xvi. 1—7.

Troubles in Israel ending in the accession of Omri; his wicked reign, ch. xvi. 8—28.

Beginning of Ahab's reign. Rebuilding of Jericho, chap. xvi. 29—34.

The history of Elijah, chaps. xvii., xviii., xix.

First invasion by Benhadad, chap. xx.

Seizure of Naboth's vineyard, the king's crime, and Elijah's denunciation, chap. xxi.

Accession, history, and death of Ahaziah, king of Israel, 1 Kings xxii. 51—53; 2 Kings i. 1—18.

Translation of Elijah; history and miracles of Elisha, 2 Kings ii., iii., (defeat of Moab) iv., v., (cure of Naaman) vi., vii., (deliverance of Samaria) viii. 1—15.

Anointing, accession, and sanguinary deeds of Jehu, 2 Kings ix., x.

III. NARRATIVES PECULIAR TO CHRONICLES.

Military preparations of Asa, 2 Chron. xiv. 6—8.

Invasion and defeat of Zerah the Ethiopian, chap. xiv. 9—15; xv. 1—7.

Great religious revival under Asa, chap. xv. 8—19.

Measures of Jehoshaphat for the instruction of the people; his military preparations and courts of justice, chap. xvii. 7—19; xix. 4—11.

Prophet's reproof of Jehoshaphat for alliance with Ahab, chap. xix. 1—3.

Attack by Moab and Ammon; the Hallelujah victory, chap. xx. 1—30.

Jehoram of Judah slays his brethren; letter of Elijah; invasion of Philistines and Arabs; the king's fatal disease and unhonoured death, chap. xxi. 2—4, 12—20.

A glance at the above will show the difference between the scope and design of the two histories. In the Kings we have the annals of *the nation*; in the Chronicles the history of the *national religion*. The latter, accordingly, is almost confined to Judah. It is a "history with a purpose,"—perhaps written by Ezra the scribe for the instruction of the Jews after the captivity; and its inspired lesson is that *so long as the people sought the Lord, He made them to prosper.*

B.—CHRONOLOGICAL DIFFICULTY IN BAASHA'S REIGN.

In 2 Chron. xvi. 1 we read that "*in the six and thirtieth year* of the reign of Asa, Baasha king of Israel came up against Judah, and built Ramah." But we find from 1 Kings xv. 33 that Baasha began his reign in the *third* year of Asa, and reigned in all *twenty-four* years; dying, therefore, in the twenty-seventh year of Asa's reign. The two statements are plainly incompatible, and the Chronicler must have counted his thirty-six years from some other starting-point, probably from the disruption. The invasion of Baasha would thus be about the fifteenth year of Asa's reign.

The above instance will illustrate the difficulty often found in reconciling the dates specified in these books. We must know the *data* of reckoning—not always easy to assign—before we can pronounce upon the method of reconciling the various statements.

C.—The Moabite Stone.

This most interesting monument of Biblical antiquity was discovered at the site of Dibon, the old Moabite city, in the year 1868. It was a block slab of basalt, 3 ft. 5 in. by 1 ft. 9 ir., containing an inscription, of which a "squeeze" or fac-simile transcript was obtained in 1869, the stone being afterwards broken up by the superstitious Arabs. The inscription has been translated as follows, the few gaps being supplied. It is wonderfully striking, as giving from the Moabitish point of view a contemporary account of the struggles of that nation with Israel. Mesha, the author, is mentioned 2 Kings iii. 4.

Translation.

"I, Mesha, son of Mehoshgad, King of Moab, the Dibonite, my father reigned over Moab thirty years, and I reigned after my father. And I made this high place for Kemosh in Korchoh, a place of deliverance, because he delivered me from all enemies, and let me look [with pleasure] upon [the destruction of] all my haters. Then arose Omri, King of Israel, and he oppressed Moab many days, because Kemosh was angry with his land. And his son [Ahab] succeeded him, and he too said, 'I will oppress Moab.' In my days he said this, but I looked upon [the ruin of] him and his house, and Israel perished for ever. And Omri had taken possession of the Plain of Medeba, and dwelt in it, and they oppressed Moab, he and his son, forty years, but looked upon him [*i.e.*, Kemosh] in my days. And I built [*i.e.*, restored or fortified] Baal-Meon, and constructed in it the moat; and I built Kirjathaim. And the men of God were dwelling in the land of Axaroth from of old, and the King of Israel had built for himself the city; and I fought against the city, and took it, and slew all the inhabitants of the city [a], a [pleasing] sight to Kemosh and to Moab; and I carried off thence the . . . . . of Jehovah, and dragged it [or them] before Kemosh at Kerioth. And I made dwell in it [viz. Axaroth] the people of Shinan and the people of M.ch.rath. And Kemosh said to me, 'Go, take Nebb from Israel;' and I went by night and fought against it from the dawning of the morning until midday, and I took it, and slew the whole [population] of it, seven thousand, ... for to Ashtor-Kemosh I had devoted it; and I took away thence the vessels of Jehovah, and dragged them before Kemosh. And the King of Israel [Amaziah] built Johaz, and abode in it while he was fighting against me; but Kemosh drove him out before me; and I took of Moab two hundred men, all his head men, and I led them up to Johaz, and took it, in addition to Dibon. I built Korchoh, the wall of the woods and the wall of the mound, and I built its gates, and I built its towers; and I built the palace, and I made the reservoirs for rain water in the midst of the city. And there was not a cistern in the midst of the city, in Korchoh; and I said to the whole people, 'Make for yourselves each a cistern in his house.' And I cut the moat for Korchoh with [the labour of] the captives of Israel. I built Aroer, and I made the road over the Arnon. I, &c. I built Beth-Bomoth, for it had been pulled down. I built Bezer, for . . . . men of Dibon, fifty [in number] for all Dibon was submissive [submissive to me]. And I . . . . . in the cities which I added to the land. And I built . . . . and Beth-Diblaim and Beth-Baal Mem; and I took up thither the . . . . . . the land. And Hormin there dwelt in it. B . . . . . . And Kemosh said to me, 'Go down, fight against Hormaim.' And I . . . . Kemosh in my days. And . . . . . . year . . . ."

D.—INTERVIEW OF HAZAEL WITH ELISHA.
2 Kings viii. 7.

Ver. 7. **Elisha came to Damascus.** There was then peace between Israel and Syria; hostilities from the side of the latter having ceased for a while after the wonderful deliverance of Samaria (chap. vii.). Elisha went, no doubt, by Divine direction.

8, 9. In the message there was implied "a tacit request from Benhadad that the prophet would obtain his recovery from Jehovah by prayer." *Bähr* [in *Lange's* series], who also remarks that it is unlikely that the prophet who had rejected Naaman's present (chap. v. 16) would accept that of Benhadad.

10. The most difficult verse in the narrative. It may be taken in one or two ways (other interpretations seem inadmissible). *First,* " Say to him, Thou shalt certainly recover (*mayest,* and *howbeit*

afterwards, are not according to the original); *i.e.*, the *disease* is not mortal—so far as that is concerned he will get well,—and [but] I know"—looking full at the hypocritical Hazael—"that he will die from another cause." Or else, *secondly*, "Say to him, Thou shalt surely *not* recover, and [for] the Lord hath showed to me," &c. The turning-point is in a matter familiar to readers of the Hebrew Scriptures. There are a few passages in which a mistaken reading, from the error of some copyist, had plainly crept into the text, but as reverence forbade the Masorite transcribers to alter it, they simply called attention to the fact, and put the true reading (or what they considered such) in the margin. The erroneous word in the text is called the *kethibh* (written), the correct reading in the margin the *keri* (read). In this particular case (and in some similar ones) the *kethibh* is "*not*" ("Say, Thou shalt surely not recover"); the *keri* is "*to him*" ("Say to him, Thou shalt surely recover"). The matter is complicated by the fact that the two words in question, though written differently, are in pronunciation exactly the same. לו *ló*, meaning *not*, and לו *ló, to him*. It is, perhaps, impossible to decide which reading is to be preferred; but it must be noted that the Masorites were occasionally mistaken, most critics adopting the interpretation (*keri*) "Say to him, Thou shalt recover." Dr. Porter gives very weighty reasons on the contrary (for the *kethibh*), "Say, Thou shalt not ;" and this appears to us on the whole the preferable construction.*

References and Authorities.

Masorites, the editors of the Hebrew Scriptures.

Kitto: Daily Scripture Illustrations.

12. These atrocities seem inseparable from Oriental guerilla warfare. There is no *direct* evidence of Hazael having done all this, only by inference from chap. x. 32—34; xiii. 3, 4, 7, 22.

Ps. cxxxvii. 9.
Isa. xiii. 15, 16
Hos. x. 14; xiii. 16.
Amos i. 13.
Nahum iii. 10.

13. This verse is generally misunderstood, as though Hazael would express his horror at the notion of committing such crimes. In fact, he is only professing a sense of personal unworthiness for so high a destiny. "What is then thy servant—the dog !—that he should do this great thing ?" The thought present to his mind is the "*great thing*"—that it will be for him to reign over Syria and lead forth its armies.

* There is an instance of a similar question between the two words in Ps. c. 3 : " It is He that hath made us, and *not* we " (ourselves) according to the *kethibh*, or, " It is He that made us, and *to Him* we " (belong) according to the *keri*. The latter seems the more natural reading.

CHAPTER IV.

THE TWO KINGDOMS DURING THE DYNASTY OF JEHU.

Israel.	Judah.
884 JEHU	*Usurpation of* ATHALIAH
Prophet *Jonah ?*	
878	JOASH or JEHOASH
	Prophet—*Joel ?*
856 JEHOAHAZ	*Repairing of the Temple.*
Ravages of the Syrians.	
840 JEHOASH, or JOASH	*Syrians invade Judah.*
Defeats the Syrians thrice.	
839	AMAZIAH.
	Conquers Edom.
Jehoash conquers Judah.	
825 JEROBOAM II.	
811	AZARIAH or UZZIAH
	Prophet—*Amos.*
784 *Interregnum*	
774 ZECHARIAH	
Slain by Shallum.	*Uzziah still reigning.*

§ 1.—JEHU AND HIS SUCCESSORS.

Jehu, King of Israel.

It would almost appear that the force of JEHU's character expended itself in that fierce outburst at the beginning of his reign; for, although he occupied the throne of Israel for eight and twenty years, the rest of his history is but the record of religious failure and diminishing empire. Jehu had uprooted Baal worship, but he himself continued in the "sins of Jeroboam." The sanctuaries at Bethel and at Dan, with their "golden calves," still remained. As the inspired historian seems to intimate, the rough warrior was religiously careless. He "took no heed"—"observed not" to walk with a whole heart in the way of the Divine law. Although the instrument of a fearful judgment on disobedience of one kind, he heedlessly fell into impiety of another; and whilst it was predicted that, in acknowledgment of his work in destroying the house of Ahab, the children of Jehu should hold the throne of Israel for four generations, there was no glory in their successive reigns until the days of the second Jeroboam.

Syrian aggressions.

Syria was now the avowed enemy of Israel, and in many a savage incursion Hazael fulfilled the sad prediction uttered years previously by Elisha. The military prowess of Jehu seems to have been utterly overmatched. The skilful plotter, the bold assassin, could not defend his own dominions. Gradually he saw them rent from his grasp. Gilead had never been fairly recovered; the southern territory of

Reuben now was seized by Syria, to Aroer on the Arnon; while the broad pastures of Bashan, extending from near Damascus to the Gileadite hills, were wrested from the children of Manasseh. The whole east of Jordan, in fact, fell under the power of Hazael.

References and Authorities.

Nor can it be doubted that the king of Syria exercised some oppressive authority even over the western territory. His seizure of Gath and threatening of Jerusalem, afterwards related, show that a way was somehow open to him through the land of Israel; and we are expressly told that "Hazael oppressed Israel all the days" of Jehu's son and successor. Meanwhile the prophet JONAH had arisen to restore the fainting hopes of Israel, and in prophecies, to which only an allusion remains, to announce a future deliverance from the Syrian yoke. The chief interest of Jonah's history rests indeed on other grounds. It is in his twofold character, as a missionary to heathen Nineveh and as a type of the "Son of Man," that we are especially to regard him. But his message to Israel was not without importance, as a link in the long series of prophetic declarations which showed that Jehovah never forgot His people, even when He smote them for their sins.

1 Kings xiv. 25.

The next king was JEHOAHAZ, son of Jehu, of whose seventeen years' reign the chief record is again that with strange infatuation he continued in the old idolatries of Jeroboam, and that the land was increasingly oppressed by Hazael, and on his death by Benhadad the Second, Hazael's son. This monarch, not content with harassing Israel in every way, laid a restriction upon their army, permitting Jehoahaz

Jehoahaz King of Israel.

References and Authorities. to retain only ten thousand infantry, with fifty horsemen and ten chariots. The land might thus become at any time an easy prey to the power of Damascus. One gleam of light indeed falls upon the character and career of this hapless king of Israel:—"Jehoahaz besought the Lord, and the Lord hearkened unto him.'' The prayer was sincere, even though associated with the degrading calf-worship; and the subsequent successes of Jehoash, and still more of Jeroboam II., against the Syrian power were a proof that Jehovah had heard the cry of the people and their king.

Joash, King of Israel.

To Jehoahaz succeeded his son JEHOASH, or JOASH,* and exercised a troubled sovereignty in Israel for sixteen years. His reign is remarkable not only for the first success against the Syrian power, but for the prophetic intimation which the aged and dying ELISHA gave of these victories. The symbolic action by which the prediction was accompanied was characteristic, if we may so say, of Elisha's *method*. With him, the word never went alone; there was also the outward act. Naaman must wash in Jordan; the salt must be cast into the bitter waters, and the meal into the pottage; the staff must be reached to the iron that it might swim. So, in the present instance, the arrow shot by Joash, "eastward," or in the direction of Syria,—a defiant act, paralleled in the custom of many nations,—is declared by the prophet to be "the arrow

2 Kings ii. 21, iv. 41; v. 10; vi. 6, &c.

---

* It may be requisite again to remark on the occurrence of the same names among the kings of Judah and of Israel. See *ante* p. 74. Joash of Judah died about the year Joash of Israel came to the throne.

of the Lord's deliverance." What follows is harder to understand. The number of victories to be won by Joash could hardly depend on the number of times he smote the ground. The act was perhaps a symbol. The king was one who stayed his hand too soon, in smaller as in greater matters; and the same tendency which led him to smite the ground only thrice would be shown in the disposition to cease the work o conquest before the hostile nation was fully subdued. The result was as predicted: Joash defeated Syria in three campaigns, and recovered the districts which Hazael and Benhadad II. had overrun. It was reserved for the greater son of Joash to push these victories further, and to extend the boundaries of Israel to the utmost extent that they ever attained. *References and Authorities.*

The short and sharp struggle between Judah and Israel, in which Joash was signally victorious, belongs rather to the history of the southern kingdom. Amaziah, the king of Judah, was the aggressor, and received but a just answer to his boastful challenge in the day when the Israelitish army advanced from Bethshemesh to Jerusalem, and not only pillaged the temple, but destroyed four hundred cubits of the city wall. The breach, no doubt, was soon repaired, but the memory of the humiliation would be ineffaceable. *Contest with Judah.*

Scanty records remain of the reign of JEROBOAM II., son and successor to Joash. He occupied the throne of Israel for forty-one years, and by his prowess not only delivered the nation effectually from the oppression of Syria, but extended its boundaries beyond any former limit. He even captured Damascus, although *Jeroboam II, King of Israel.*

Compare 2 Sam. viii. 5, 6—9. 1 Kings viii. 65.

most probably contenting himself with asserting his supremacy at its gates, and requiring, according to former precedent, that "streets," or an Israelitish quarter, might be granted him in that city. Jeroboam also secured Hamath on the Orontes, the key to Eastern Syria, thus repeating the achievements of David and Solomon, who had held that strong position in the days when the supremacy of Judah was unquestioned in Israel. The weakness of Syria at this juncture may excite surprise; it was probably due in part to the growing might of Assyria, which was beginning to push its conquests beyond the Euphrates, and in another generation was to make not only Syria but Israel its prey.

References and Authorities.

See prediction of Amos, i. 3—5.

The revival of Israelite power was, however, only temporary; Jeroboam II. had steadfastly maintained the worship instituted by his namesake; and the steadfast refusal of Israel, prolonged now through so many generations, to recognise its divine calling, and to pursue the path of obedience, could not but issue in weakness and final overthrow. The deliverance of the people from its oppressors by the hand of Jeroboam is assigned, in touching language, to the tender pity of Jehovah: well would it have been for king and people had they laid the lesson to heart! As it was, Zachariah the son of Jeroboam inherited his father's godlessness, but not his courage, his greatness, nor his success. It was only after an interregnum, and no doubt much severe though unrecorded civil struggle, that he obtained possession of the throne, and when at last his royalty was acknowledged he reigned

Zachariah, son of Jeroboam.

See Note C.

but for six months, falling by the hand of an assassin, one "Shallum, son of Jabesh." Thus passed away the line of Jehu, after having afforded in its chequered but for the most part inglorious history a melancholy comment on the boastful words of its founder, *Come, see my zeal for the Lord of hosts.*

<small>*References and Authorities.* End of the house of Jehu. See prediction of Amos, viii. 9</small>

§ 2.—ACCESSION AND REIGN OF JOASH IN JUDAH.

The seven years which followed the death of Ahaziah may count among the saddest periods of Judæan history. To all appearance the line of David was extinct, and the act of an idolatrous queen had frustrated the purposes of God! The "lamp" ordained for the "anointed" of Jehovah had been quenched in darkness; and the prophets were found false witnesses for God! One infant life, however, secretly preserved, was to continue the great succession, and to prove that the Most High had not suffered His faithfulness to fail.

<small>Melancholy prospects.</small>

Jehoiada the high priest had married Jehosheba, the daughter of Jehoram, king of Judah, most probably by a former marriage; half-sister, therefore, of the slain Ahaziah. In the slaughter of the royal children by their grandmother, the youngest, JOASH, was taken by this aunt of his, and concealed in a store-room of the high priest's house. Athaliah meanwhile reigned securely, unaware of the elements of ruin which were gathering so near. The infant prince was after a while removed with his nurse to one of the apartments in the temple, where he could remain unsuspected among the children of the Levites.

<small>Preservation of Joash. 2 Chron. xx. 2.</small>

"And Athaliah did reign over the land." The six years of her usurped sway must have been a time of strange terror in Judah. The worship of Baal, suppressed in Samaria, was transferred to Jerusalem. The survivors of Jehu's massacres would naturally flee to the daughter of Jezebel; and the idol of the Phœnicians soon had a temple, altars, images, priesthood, in the city of God. Yet no active measures of reprisal seem to have been taken by the idolatrous queen. We read of no proscription or persecution in Judah, of no movement against Israel. Nor did Athaliah dare to touch the Levitical priesthood, still less to desecrate the temple of Jehovah. She had, indeed, in the lifetime of her husband, to some extent despoiled the house of God of its treasures and "dedicated things," her sons before their melancholy end having been her coadjutors. But now the services of the sanctuary were continued without hindrance or molestation. The votaries of the two religions were driven by mutual fear to mutual tolerance; while the Levites, as representing the popular traditions and hopes, would acquire new influence; the centre of gravity of the nation, so to speak, being gradually but finally transferred to the ecclesiastical authority. Now, especially "in the absence of any representative of David, there was nothing else round which the nation could rally; so that Jehoiada at this moment was little less than an Eli to it."

Before the moment for action had arrived, Jehoiada had made sure of the fidelity of the royal guard, and had apprised the Levites throughout Judah of his purpose. Some obscurity hangs over the details; chiefly from the different points of view taken in the two accounts. Thus much, however, is plain, that the time chosen for the decisive blow was the Sabbath, when two bands of Levites could assemble in the temple without suspicion, those who were finishing their term of attendance being detained with those who had arrived to succeed them. There seems to have been also a military guard of the temple, and by fixing upon the hour of changing sentries, this force likewise would be doubled. In addition to these, the members of the royal guard could freely enter the temple courts with the general congregation; but, to disarm suspicion, they were directed to come without weapons, a supply being provided from the temple arsenal. The measures of Jehoiada were so promptly and effectively taken that at the appointed hour every entrance to the building, as well as to the queen's palace, was occupied in force, while a strong bodyguard surrounded the young prince as he came forth, led by the high priest, and was placed on the elevated spot, "by the pillar," at the summit of the steps leading from the outer to the inner court, where royalty was accustomed to take its stand. There was no time for questioning or wonder. As soon as the youthful Joash appeared, a trumpet blast rung through the temple. Jehoiada placed the crown upon his head, anointed him with the consecrated oil, and delivered into his hands the scroll of Jehovah's law. Those who were in the secret, scattered through the multitude, raised the shout, "God save the king!"

References and Authorities.

The Sabbath now first mentioned in the history of the Monarchy.

Names of the leaders, 2 Chron. xxiii. 1.

2 Kings xxiii. 3.
2 Chron. xxxiv. 31.
See 2 Chron. vi. 13.

The "Testimony."
Exod. xvi. 34
xxv. 21;
Deut. xvii. 19.
1 Kings i. 25.

References and Authorities. The gathered concourse caught the impulsive fervour, apprehended in an instant the true condition of affairs, and united in the joyous cry.

Fate of Athaliah. Soon the noise of the shouting reached the royal apartments. Brave, like her mother, the queen hastened to the scene. A glance revealed all. She rent her clothes, exclaiming, "Treason! treason!" but none rallied to her side. Jehoiada gave the signal; she was hurried through the ranks of the people, and slain outside the temple. The revolution was completed in this decisive blow. No defence was attempted by the party of Baal; and the only life that was further taken was that of Mattan, the high priest of Baal, who (as the people rushed to destroy the idol temple) was slain before the shrine.

Reign of Joash. The scanty records that remain of the long reign of Joash show him to have been a prince of fine impulses, but easily led by his advisers, and lacking moral courage. So long as Jehoiada survived, the king was true to the God of his fathers. In his youthful enthusiasm he devoted himself to the restoration of the temple after the spoliations of Athaliah; but whether from laxity on the part of Jehoiada, or from the king's own weakness in enforcing his com-
Temple repairs. mands, the contribution levied for the purpose languished for many years. Little more, in fact, seems to have been collected than sufficed for the priests' own maintenance, while the accounts were kept with a laxity that exposed the ecclesiastical body to suspicion. It was the twenty-third year of Joash before efficient arrangements were made for the purpose.

The work then went on expeditiously; contributors being liberal, and craftsmen enthusiastic, as well as faithful in their allotted tasks. On this occasion, and in a similar work of later days, the striking record is made that no account was taken from the men to whom the outlay was entrusted, for "they dealt faithfully." The apostle Paul has shown us what is perhaps the higher rule of Christian prudence in such matters, by submitting to the strictest scrutiny the details of the benevolent fund which he administered; but it is impossible not to admire on the one hand the scrupulous fidelity of these Jewish workmen, and on the other the simple trust of their employers. The temple no doubt required a thorough renovation. Quite apart from the mischiefs wrought by Athaliah, the dilapidations of so large a building, which had now stood for a hundred and fifty years, would be very serious. But large as was the sum required for repairs, the contribution was considerably in excess; and the surplus was devoted, by the order of Jehoiada and the king, to replacing the gold and silver vessels of the sanctuary, which at the outset had been omitted from the estimate.

References and Authorities.

2 Kings xii. 15; xxii. 7

2 Cor. viii. 20, 21.

Temple dedicated B.C. 1,004. Repairs by Joash completed about B.C. 854.

Thus were the ancient honours of the temple renewed; and so long as Jehoiada lived, the king and people statedly and to all appearance heartily united in its solemnities.

But the national reformation was to a great extent unreal. Secretly, the fascinations of Baal-worship were still felt by many, and its rites no doubt were practised. Not all the efforts of the great priest, seconded as they were by the influence of the king, could induce

"Burnt offerings continually," 2 Chron. xxiv. 14. Baalite reaction.

References and Authorities. the people to forsake the local centres of worship, and to restrict at least the offering of burnt sacrifice and incense to Jerusalem. The "high places" remained in the land; and the authorities were compelled to tolerate these irregular sanctuaries, which naturally became centres of will worship, and, in the sequel, of a worse idolatry. Joash was too weak to resist, Jehoiada was probably inert through age and infirmity. On the death of the latter, at the age of one hundred and thirty, the secular and irreligious elements, subdued during the period of Levitical ascendency, again appeared. The courtiers of Judah set themselves once more with effect against the priesthood, and by their adulation won the feeble king to their side. Permission was given to re-institute the worship of Baal and Ashtoreth, and once more there were rival sanctuaries in the city of God. The fact was the more ominous of evil because it was a *reaction.* Had the popular enthusiasm for the restoration of the temple, then, been a mere pretence? Was it not time for another Elijah to arise and say to the men of Judah also, "How long halt ye between two opinions? If Baal be God, then obey him; but if Jehovah be God, then obey Him"?

See Jer. vii. 25, 26. Jonah was (probably) a little earlier. Joel and Amos later. Zachariah. Matt. xxiii. 35. "Son of Barachias." See Note.

In this crisis prophets did appear, all save one of unrecorded name. What their message was we cannot doubt; it was wickedly disregarded. Foremost among the witnesses for God stood one of whom we know but little, but whose name has the imperishable honour of a mention by Christ himself as representative of the martyr band. ZACHARIAH the priest, son and successor of Jehoiada, assuming by divine command the attitude and tone of a prophet, stood forth to protest against the general apostasy. The people made answer in the old fanatic fashion, the king himself approving their deed. "They stoned Zachariah with stones that he died." He fell "in the court of the house of the Lord," "between the temple and the altar;" and as he sank beneath the shower of stones he cried, "The Lord look upon it and require it." Ages afterwards another witness to the truth was to yield up his life in the same manner, almost in the same place, exclaiming with his dying breath, "Lord, lay not this sin to their charge." The contrast between the last words of Zachariah and those of Stephen may measure for us the difference between the Jewish and the Christian dispensations. *[margin: References and Authorities.]* *[margin: Acts vii. 60.]*

To the sin of departure from God, Joash had now added the basest ingratitude to the memory of the man who had preserved his infant life and raised him to the throne. It is no wonder that his later years were marked by disaster and misery. The Syrians under Hazael, whose exploits against Israel have been noted in the previous section, swooped down upon Jerusalem, having made themselves masters of Gath and the western coast. Already possessing the territory east of Jordan, they now hemmed in the land of Judah, to all appearance hopelessly. Their army, we are expressly told, was small; that of Joash was far greater; but the Syrians were decisively victorious, it would seem, in some general engagement, which so opened up the way to the Judæan capital, *[margin: Syrian inroads.]*

References and Authorities. that Joash was compelled to purchase the evacuation of his territory with the treasures of the Temple added to his own. So speedily were lost for ever the rich stores which in the earlier part of this reign had been brought willingly and rejoicingly by the people into the house of God! They had forsaken Him, and had thus made the very gifts which they had brought to Him before, as an accursed thing! It was a small matter that the silver and the gold should be swept off to a heathen land, for the heart of the people had turned to Baal first.

Death of Joash. Joash appears to have been wounded in the encounter with the Syrians, and as he was lying in great consequent feebleness at Beth-millo, two of his servants slew him on his bed. Their conspiracy is connected by the Chronicler with "the blood of the sons of Jehoiada the priest," as though the act were in some way prompted by vengeance for the death of Zachariah. This, however, is uncertain. Joash was the first prince of the house of David who fell by assassination; his strange and wilful departure from God had already cast over his reign a dark shadow, and he remains a warning to all ages to those who are kept for a time in the right path by the influence of others, or by the force of circumstances, without any deeply inwrought principle or conviction. Remove the prop, and they will too surely fail.

"The house of the Millo," apparently near Jerusalem. See p. 9.

The horror of the regicidal act—unprecedented in Judah, although so unhappily familiar in Israel—is partially lightened by the fact that the conspirators were both of alien blood; one being the son of an

The conspirators.

Ammonite mother, the other of a Moabitess. Joash passed away unlamented and without honour, being refused a place in the sepulchres of the kings—perhaps because of his having fallen by a violent death.

<small>*References and Authorities.* Zabad (or Jozachar) son of Shimeath (or Shomer).</small>

§ 3.—Reign of Amaziah.

Jehoiada the priest had taken for Joash two wives—so dependent had this king been from the first upon his great adviser! One of them was Jehoaddan of Jerusalem, whose son Amaziah began to reign at the age of twenty-five, having been born therefore when his father was twenty-two years old. It is not often that the chronological and personal *data* are given with such particularity.

<small>Wives of Joash—his heir.</small>

One of the first acts of Amaziah, when in secure possession of the throne, was to execute justice upon the assassins of his father. This was but natural; there was, however, in the manner of the deed a most noteworthy departure from former precedent, in obedience to the law of God. Hitherto it had seemed almost a matter of course that the children of a malefactor should suffer with him the consequence of his crime. But Amaziah had learned to read the divine law for himself, interpreting it by its own light, apart from tradition or convention. This then he found written:—"The fathers shall not be put to death for the children, neither shall the children be put to death for the fathers: every man shall be put to death for his own sin." On this principle he acted; and the incident is memorable, not only as illustrating the justice of God's law, but as a very early recognition

<small>Amaziah's first acts.</small>

<small>Deut. xxiv. 16.</small>

References and Authorities.
Isa. viii. 20.

of the principle afterwards embodied by Isaiah in the proverbial saying, "To the law and to the testimony." We have seen that at the coronation of Joash "the testimony" was placed in his hands by Jehoiada; and we cannot doubt that with the progress of general enlightenment the Book of God became more and more a cherished possession in the palaces and homes of Judah.

Character of Amaziah.

This king Amaziah throughout his career seems only just to fall short of high excellence. There was a brilliancy in his exploits, but not without a stain of cruelty; and his energy and bravery were alloyed by a spirit of boastfulness which led to the greatest disaster of his reign. His earlier endeavours were directed to restore, so far as possible, the *prestige* of his kingdom after the blow inflicted on it by Hazael. To this end he instituted a census, summoning all capable of bearing arms to enrol themselves. As the result, he could count upon an army of 300,000 men from Judah and Benjamin, a total greatly inferior to the forces mustered by king Asa, but sufficient to prove the elasticity of the kingdom after its late heavy reverses. With this force he planned the great expedition of his reign, that against "the rock-land" beyond the Dead Sea, "Sela," the fastness of the children of Edom, or Idumæa,—the fortress city whose ruins, under the later name of *Petra*, are still the astonishment of travellers. Penetrating into this wild region—perhaps only as a security to Judah on the eastern side, perhaps with a view to further conquests—he completely routed

Compare 2 Chron. xiv. 8.

Petra.

the Edomites, and not content with his victory, or the number of the slain, cruelly killed a vast number of them in cold blood by casting them down from the rocky heights of that wild region. So wonderful did this conquest seem that the king called the place *Joktheel*, "subdued by God," acknowledging that no other power could have prevailed against it. *References and Authorities. Ten thousand. 2 Chron. xxv. 12.*

Returning to Jerusalem, Amaziah found the kingdom exposed to new difficulties; for at the outset of his Idumæan expedition he had sought to strengthen his army by enlisting from the land of Israel a host of mercenaries, 100,000 strong, the sum paid for their services being a hundred talents of silver. Against the whole proceeding a prophet, divinely commissioned, had uttered a solemn protest: the children of Ephraim must not be permitted to join in this enterprise with the men of Judah; defeat would be the certain consequence; and when the king asked the very natural question, how he was to have compensation for the hundred talents of silver, the prophet's was the answer of faith, "The Lord is able to give thee much more than this." Accordingly, the Israelite troops were disbanded; but they would naturally be exasperated at being thus cast off; and during the absence of Amaziah on his expedition they fell upon many of the towns of Judah that lay in their homeward track, slaying the inhabitants and carrying off much booty. *Difficulties with Israel.*

Nor was this great political mistake the only error of the king. Flushed with victory over the Edomites, he led their deities also in triumph, and like the *Adoption of Edomite gods.*

Romans of a later date, appropriated them by right of conquest. It is difficult to understand the reasoning by which a prince, who had learned from the law that Jehovah was sole monarch of the nations, could justify the adoption in any way of "other gods." They were probably held by Amaziah to be tutelary divinities of Edom, of proved inferiority to the God of Israel, but to be treated with some sort of respect as conquered spiritual enemies that might one day become formidable, and whose favour it was at least worth while to secure. Hence he bowed himself before these gods and burned incense to them. A prophet of God, again of unknown name, was courageous enough to protest against this strange impiety, meeting the king on his own ground, and arguing that, as these gods could not save their own nation, it must be futile to adore them. The haughty king could not brook the interference; and the prophet accepted the royal mandate which doomed him to be silent. "The prophet forbare," and left Amaziah to his wilfulness and to his doom.

In Israel king Joash was now reigning, and Amaziah, no doubt exasperated by the aggressions of the disbanded Israelite mercenaries, as well as lifted up with pride after his Edomite conquests, challenged him to a trial of strength: "Come, let us look one another in the face." The reply of Joash was in the form of a fable, expressive and contemptuous, with a yet more scornful application. "But Amaziah would not hear." The armies of Judah and of Israel therefore met in fratricidal strife at Beth-shemesh. Joash achieved an easy victory over his boastful challenger; *References and Authorities.* but, with a curious mixture of scorn and forbearance, contented himself with leading Amaziah back as a prisoner of war to Jerusalem, reinstating him there upon his throne, and leaving as the only token of the conquest the wall of the city broken down " from the gate of Ephraim unto the corner gate, four hundred cubits,"—despoiling also the palace and temple of the treasures that Hazael had suffered to remain, or that had been accumulated since the Syrian invasion, doubtless including the spoils of Edom. Having thus effectively humbled the pride of Judah, Joash returned to Samaria with hostages that the peace between the two kingdoms should no more be similarly broken. But the precaution was unnecessary. Amaziah was humbled by the hand of God, and seems to have so far profited by the discipline of adversity, that we read of no more attempted achievements. The latter part of his reign—and he survived his antagonist Joash fifteen years—is quite unnoted. That newly-built portion of the wall of Jerusalem would always disgrace him in the eyes of his subjects. The end was a conspiracy: he fled to Lachish, but was pursued and slain,—resembling his father in his fate, and terminating ingloriously what might once have promised to be a splendid and distinguished reign.

The great career of UZZIAH was only in part con- *Accession of Uzziah.* temporaneous with the dynasty of Jehu: it may therefore be most conveniently considered under another division of the history. Suffice it here to say that while Jeroboam II. was enlarging the boundaries of

References and Authorities. Israel and reclaiming the territories that had been overrun by Syria, Uzziah was, with equal success, taking measures to protect and strengthen the boundaries of Judah. Both kingdoms for a while were strong in internal resources and outward defence; and the only cloud in the distance was that which eventually was to spread until it darkened the heavens —the growing power of Assyria.

NOTES TO CHAPTER IV.
A.—THE PARALLEL ACCOUNTS.
I. NARRATIVES COMMON TO KINGS AND CHRONICLES.

The Accession of Joash; death of Athaliah, 2 Kings xi. 4—20; 2 Chron. xxiii. Substantially the same account, save that the Chronicles is careful to specify the part that the Levites had in the transaction; see especially ver. 6, to which there is nothing in Kings to correspond; also the amplification in ver. 18. **General outline of the reign of Joash,** 2 Kings xi. 21; xii. 1—5; 2 Chron. xxiv. 1—3. The latter adds the reference to the two wives whom Jehoiada took for him; the former notes the continued existence of the "high places."

Repair of the temple under Joash, 2 Kings xii. 6—16; 2 Chron. xxiv. 4—14. These are plainly independent accounts of the same transactions.

Troubles in the latter part of his reign from Syria, 2 Kings xii. 17, 18; 2 Chron. xxiv. 23, 24; independent narratives, subjoined for comparison.

KINGS.

"Then Hazael king of Syria went up, and fought against Gath, and took it: and Hazael set his face to go up to Jerusalem. And Jehoash king of Judah took all the hallowed things that Jehoshaphat, and Jehoram, and Ahaziah, his fathers, kings of Judah, had dedicated, and his own hallowed things, and all the gold that was found in the treasures of the house of the Lord, and in the king's house, and sent it to Hazael, king of Syria: and he went away from Jerusalem."

CHRONICLES.

"And it came to pass at the end of the year, that the host of Syria came up against him: and they came to Judah and Jerusalem, and destroyed all the princes of the people from among the people, and sent all the spoil of them unto the king of Damascus. For the army of the Syrians came with a small company of men, and the Lord delivered a very great host into their hand, because they had forsaken the Lord God of their fathers. So they executed judgment againt Joash."

Conspiracy and murder of the king, 2 Kings xii. 19—21; 2 Chron. xxiv. 25—27; independent accounts subjoined.

KINGS.

"And the rest of the acts of Joash, and all that he did, are they not written in the book of the chronicles of the kings of Judah? And his servants arose, and made a conspiracy, and slew Joash in the house of Millo, which goeth down to Silla. For Jozachar the son of Shimeath, and Jehozabad the son of Shomer, his servants, smote him, and he died; and they buried him with his fathers in the city of David: and Amaziah his son reigned in his stead."

CHRONICLES.

"And when they were departed from him (for they left him in great diseases), his own servants conspired against him for the blood of the sons of Jehoiada the priest, and slew him on his bed, and he died: and they buried him in the city of David, but they buried him not in the sepulchres of the kings. And these are they that conspired against him; Zabad the son of Shimeath an Ammonitess, and Jehozabad the son of Shimrith a Moabitess. Now concerning his sons, and the greatness of the burdens laid upon him, and the repairing of the house of God, behold, they are written in the story of the book of the kings. And Amaziah his son reigned in his stead."

Accession and reign of Amaziah, 2 Kings xiv. 1—6; 2 Chron. xxv. 1—10. Substantially the same account, it being however added in Kings that "the high places were not taken away," ver. 4.

Expedition against the Edomites, 2 Kings xiv. 7; 2 Chron. xxv. 11, 12.; Independent notices the former gives the name (Selah, Joktheel, Petra), the latter adds the inci-

dent of the casting down of the ten thousand captives from "the rock."

Challenge of Amaziah to Joash of Israel; defeat and humiliation of the former, 2 Kings xiv. 8—14; 2 Chron. xxv. 17—24. The same document with slight variations; the latter adding the moral of Amaziah's defeat: "It came of God, that He might deliver them into the hand of their enemies, because they sought after the gods of Edom."

Amaziah slain in a conspiracy, 2 Kings xiv. 17—20; 2 Chron. xxv. 25—28; the same narrative, save that the Chronicles adds that the catastrophe was "after the time that Amaziah did turn away from following the Lord."

Accession of Azariah or Uzziah, and capture of Elath, 2 Kings xiv. 21, 22; 2 Chron. xxvi. 1., 2. The same paragraph.

II. SECTIONS PECULIAR TO THE KINGS.

Aggressions of Syria in the days of Jehu; his death, 2 Kings x. 32, 36.

Reign of Jehoahaz, king of Israel, chap. xiii. 1—9.

Reign of Joash, or Jehoash, in Israel, chap. xiii. 10—13, 22—24.

Death of Elisha, &c., chap. xiii. 14—21.

Three victories of Joash over Syria, chap. xiii. 25.

Death of Joash of Israel, chap. xiii. 12, 13; xiv. 15, 16. This paragraph is singularly given twice in the same book.

Reign of Jeroboam II., chap. xiv. 23—27.

III. SECTIONS PECULIAR TO THE CHRONICLES.

Death of Jehoiada, 2 Chron. xxiv. 15, 16.

Idolatry of Joash in Judah; martyrdom of Zechariah, chap. xxiv. 17—22.

Amaziah's levy of Israelite troops; their dismission and ravages, chap. xxv. 5—10, 13.

Amaziah worships the Edomite gods, chap. xxv. 14—16.

Details of Uzziah's reign, chap. xxvi. (See next chapter.)

B.—DIFFICULTIES IN DATES, AND SUGGESTED INTERREGNUM,
p. 96.

Amaziah, king of Judah, reigned twenty-nine years (2 Kings xiv. 2). Jeroboam II. of Israel came to the throne in the fifteenth year of Amaziah (ver. 23), and reigned forty-one years, *i.e.*, fourteen years during Amaziah's lifetime, and twenty-seven years after his death. Uzziah, therefore, the successor of Amaziah, would come to the throne of Judah in the fifteenth. year of Jeroboam. But it was in the twenty-seventh year of Jeroboam (2 Kings xv. 1) that Uzziah began to reign. Again, as Jeroboam lived twenty-seven years into the reign of Uzziah, Zachariah, the successor of Jeroboam, would become king of Israel in Uzziah's twenty-eighth year. But we read of his accession in Uzziah's thirty-eighth year (2 Kings xv. 8). These difficulties are perhaps insoluble, in the absence of some of the *data*. One way of accounting for them, generally accepted and quite sufficient, is to suppose (1) That Jeroboam II. actually began to reign in conjunction with Joash his father twelve years before the death of the latter. This explains 2 Kings xv. 1. (2) That after the death of Jeroboam there was an interregnum of ten years, at the close of which Zachariah succeeded in obtaining the throne, only to lose it again almost immediately. (3) But, as there is no mention of an interregnum in history, Bähr and others suppose that a mistake has crept into the record of Jeroboam's years, the true number being not 41 but 51.

C.—THE PARABLE OF JOASH.
2 Kings xiv. 9.

"The Oriental use of apologues on the most solemn and serious occasions is well known to all. and scarcely needs illustration. The parable of Jotham is the first recorded instance, Judg. ix. 8—15. Another celebrated example is the reply of Cyrus to the Greeks of Asia, Herodotus i. 141. A third will be found in the history of Astyages."—"Ancient Monarchies," vol. iii., p. 226.

"It is a common feature of such apologues that they are not exact parallels to the case whereto they are applied, but only general or partial resemblances. Hence there is need of caution in applying the several points of the illustration."—Canon Rawlinson, *Spk. Com.*

"The main point is the contrast of the largest, strongest, and most majestic tree, the cedar, and the contemptible, weak, and useless, although prickly brier (not *thistle*). It is more a proverb than a parable. The words, *Give thy daughter to my son to wife*, are not to be interpreted as implying that Amaziah had demanded a daughter of Joash as a wife for one of his sons (as some); nor is the explanation that the kingdom of Israel is the daughter and the kingdom of Judah the son (as others), a fit interpretation of the haughty parable of the king of Israel."—Bähr, in *Lange's Series*.

D.—PROPHETS DURING THE DYNASTY OF JEHU.

During the hundred and ten years now under review, the prophetic spirit was manifested in new and even higher forms than heretofore, and its utterances began to clothe themselves in a literary and permanent shape. It is true that the prophets of Israel and Judah were no longer wonder-workers, as Elijah and Elisha had been. The need of miracle had passed away with the decisive establishment of the truth which miracles were wrought to confirm; and when the supremacy of Jehovah had been fully attested, the "mighty work" might well be succeeded by the "mighty word."

It is from the prophets that we are to gather the clearest view not only of the general course of events, as sketched in the history, but of the national character, and more especially of the national sins. It is but a narrow view of the prophetic function that regards it as only or chiefly concerned with things to come. The prophet was the moral and spiritual instructor of the people: his office was, as the very name denotes, to tell *forth*, as well as to tell *beforehand*, the counsels of the Most High. The predictive element, it is true, is never wholly absent; Joel, Amos, and Hosea, the three great prophets of this era, declare in no uncertain terms the glories of the future. But still their chief concern is with the present, as, in graphic delineation, or scathing rebuke, they expose the evils of the time.

The following are the great prophets of the epoch:—

I. ISRAEL.

1. *Jonah*, son of Amittai (2 Kings xiv. 25), predicted the restoration of the ancient boundaries of Israel. The book called by his name, narrating his expedition to Nineveh and consequent

events, is the most ancient of the prophetic canon. *Reign of Jeroboam II.*

2. *Hosea*, son of Beeri, prophesied from the days of Jeroboam II. to those of Hezekiah in Judah, being a duration, at the very least, of fifty-six years. His extant prophecies are chiefly descriptions of the idolatry and moral corruption which in his time overspread the nation, with pathetic entreaties to " Ephraim " to return to God.

II. JUDAH.

1. *Joel*, the son of Pethuel, is perhaps the oldest prophetic writer of the southern kingdom. The age in which he flourished is, however, mainly a matter of inference; chiefly from the fact that the enemies of Judah mentioned by him are Phœnicians, Philistines, Edomites, and Egyptians, no reference being made to Syria, Assyria, or to Babylon. The date, therefore, held to be most probable is that of the early days of Joash (B.C. 870—865). "The delivery of his prophecy was occasioned by the devastations produced by successive swarms of locusts, and by an excessive drought which pervaded the country and threatened the inhabitants with utter destruction. This calamity, however, was merely symbolical of another and a more dreadful scourge—the invasion of the land by foreign enemies, on which the prophet expatiates in the second chapter. In order that such calamity might be removed, he is commissioned to order a universal fast, and call all to repentance and humiliation before God; to announce, as consequent upon such repentance and humiliation, a period of great temporal prosperity; to predict the effusion of the Holy Spirit at a future period of the history of this people; to denounce judgments against their enemies, and to foretell their restoration from the final dispersion."—*Henderson.*

If Hosea is the most rugged and obscure, Joel is the most lucid and elegant of the Hebrew prophets.

2. *Amos*, shepherd of Tekoah (a little town of Judah about twelve miles south-east of Jerusalem), was called to the prophetic office as he followed the flock (vii. 15). He himself gives the date of his ministry;—the reigns of Uzziah in Judah, and Jeroboam II. in Israel, or about B.C. 811—784. The "earthquake," chap. i. 1, also referred to Zech. xiv. 5, was evidently an extraordinary visitation, but its date is unknown. Jewish writers pretend that it happened at the moment of Uzziah's sacrilege,

2 Chron. xxvi. Though a native of Judah, his chief errand was to the northern kingdom, his visit to Jeroboam's court being described with great vividness, chap. vii. 10—17. He utters predictions against the Syrians, Philistines, Phœnicians, Edomites, Ammonites, and Moabites, as well as against the Israelites and Jews. He denounces, in language instinct with rough energy and with much rustic imagery befitting his former vocation, the idolatries and sins of the people, but ends with a glowing prediction of Messianic times, chap. ix. 11; Acts xv. 16, 17.

These names by no means exhaust the great prophetic roll. See 2 Chron. xxiv. 19: "He sent prophets to them, to bring them again unto the Lord; and they testified against them, but they would not give ear." Of these only one is mentioned, Zachariah, son of Jehoiada, and as it would appear both priest and prophet. He is called by our Lord, "son of Barachias," which may have been another name of Jehoiada; or the words may have been a marginal addition by some transcriber who confounded this Zachariah with the later prophet of the same name, who was son of Berechiah (Zech. i. 1). In Isaiah viii. 2 another Zachariah (perhaps the father-in-law of Ahaz, 2 Kings xviii. 2) appears as the son of Jeberechiah.

CHAPTER V.

THE TWO KINGDOMS TO THE FALL OF THE ISRAELITE MONARCHY.

B.C.	Israel.	Judah.
773	SHALLUM	UZZIAH reigning Prophet, *Amos*
	MENAHEM Invasion by Pul	
762	PEKAHIAH	
760	PEKAH	
759	Alliance with Rezin of Syria War with Judah Invasion by Tiglath-pileser	JOTHAM Prophets, *Micah* *Isaiah*
743		AHAZ Prophets, *Isaiah* *Oded*
730	HOSHEA Alliance sought with Egypt	
727		HEZEKIAH Prophet, *Isaiah*
724	Invasion by Shalmaneser	
721	Fall of Samaria End of the monarchy *Israel in Exile.*	*Hezekiah reigning*

§ 1.—KINGDOM OF ISRAEL TO THE DEATH OF PEKAH.

Josephus.

King SHALLUM is to us a name and nothing more. After smiting down the last representative of Jehu's house, he himself "reigned a month of days in Samaria." Raised by successful treason to this brief elevation, he was conspired against in turn, and had hardly taken possession of the throne when the commander-in-chief, MENAHEM, the son of Gadi, marched from Tirzah at the head of his soldiery, slew Shallum, and reigned in his stead.

1 Kings xv. 24.

It was not to be expected that the throne of the military usurper would be peaceful or secure. The earliest annals of his reign are a record of foul barbarities exercised against those who withstood him. Tiphsah,* the scene of the worst of these atrocities, may possibly have been the city on the Euphrates afterwards known as Thapsacus, the former limit of Solomon's dominions to the north-east. Menahem, it would thus appear, was ambitiously endeavouring to regain the territories of which Israel had been long dispossessed; but the attempt brought him face to face with the growing power of Assyria, of which nation we now first read in the sacred history, after the days of Asshur. Pul, the Assyrian king, attacked the dominions of Menahem in the first of that series of inroads which ended in the utter destruction of the monarchy. For the time the forbearance of the invader was purchased by a tribute of a thousand

Gen. x. 11.

See Note B.

---

* Tiphsah = "the Ford," may, however, refer to some place nearer Tirzah.

talents, or three million shekels of silver. This vast <small>*References and Authorities.*</small> sum was raised by a forced contribution from the wealthier classes of Israel, of fifty shekels per head; the levy therefore extending to sixty thousand persons. The transaction made Israel virtually a tributary of the Assyrian power, and so prepared the way for the final catastrophe. Nothing more is recorded of Menahem, save that, unlike his predecessor and his successor, he died a natural death, being peacefully succeeded by his son PEKAHIAH.

The new king did not long enjoy the throne. After two years, in which he displayed the same evil propensities as his fathers, he was slain, and succeeded by Pekah, son of Remaliah, a general in his army. The details of the conspiracy and murder are briefly given in the history. Pekah was accompanied by fifty Gileadites, his stalwart body-guard. Two courtiers, <small>1 Chron. xii. 8; xxvi. 31.</small> Argob and Arieh, no doubt resisting the forcible entry of the conspirators, were slain with their king. Pekahiah himself had fled to the inner apartments, <small>The "palace," or "citadel."</small> probably the harem of his palace, whither he was pursued, and where he was put to death.

No opposition seems to have been attempted to the accession of PEKAH, who exercised a troubled sovereignty for twenty, or perhaps thirty years. The one act of this king that led to the subsequent disasters and overthrow of Israel was his entering into a league with Rezin, king of Syria, against the Judæan monarchy. Which of these monarchs originated the scheme is doubtful; it is easier to conjecture the political end in view. Assyria was still a growing power; Rezin and

Pekah were virtual though reluctant vassals. The ambition of the Assyrian monarch was concentrated on Egypt; but the way from the Tigris to the Nile was by Damascus, Samaria, and Jerusalem. There seemed no hope of resisting the aggression but by the consolidation of the three powers into a great confederacy; but to this policy the house of David was of necessity opposed. That royal line had ever stood, and must, by divine ordinance, remain apart from the kingdoms of the world, until its sacred destiny should be fulfilled. Unable therefore to effect the desired alliance, Israel and Syria formed the audacious scheme of dethroning the descendant of David, and placing on the throne of Judah a creature of their own, "son of Tabeal," unnamed in the inspired record, but according to some Egyptologists called *Ashariah* on the monuments.

References and Authorities.

Isa. vii. 6.

The first attack of the confederate power on the armies of Judah was terribly successful. A hundred and twenty thousand fell in one day, a prince of the blood, Maaseiah, being slain, with two of the chief nobles of the court. Multitudes were carried captive by the Syrians to Damascus; and another great body, comprising many women and children, with vast spoil, was led by the Israelites to the gates of Samaria. A new affliction was thus added to the sorrows which had befallen the land of Judah—nothing less than the threatened slavery of her children to their brethren of Israel! By the wise and courageous words of the prophet Oded this coming calamity was averted. At the very gates of the city he met the victorious army with

Azrikam and Elkanah.

their captive train, and by his energetic protest and bold reproof turned the conquerors from their purpose. If Judah and Jerusalem had sinned, and deserved humiliation, had not Ephraim and Samaria? "*Hear ye therefore, and deliver the captives again, which ye have taken captive of your brethren; for the fierce wrath of the Lord is upon you.*" Encouraged by the prophet's words, several from among the chief men of Ephraim gave their earnest counsel in the same direction; and so effectual were their representations, that the warriors relinquished their prisoners and the spoil to the care of the Samaritan community, who at once organized a band for the relief of the great company of sufferers, provided clothes and food from the booty, with means of conveyance for the feeble, and brought them to "Jericho, the city of palm trees," on the frontier of the Judæan kingdom, whence they could easily travel to Jerusalem, themselves returning to Samaria. There is scarcely a more beautiful incident in the annals of this often fratricidal warfare; and the proof is as welcome as it must have been unexpected, that in the long estrangement of these kingdoms, Israel, though the more rebellious and guilty of the two, had not forgotten the greatness of Jehovah's name, nor the sanctity of the fraternal tie.

References and Authorities.

See Lev xxv. 42—46.

This beautiful episode, however, did not end the war; and in order to renew the contest with effect, the king of Judah, in the teeth of prophetic warning, invoked the aid of Tiglath-pileser, "lord of the Tigris," second of that name according to the monuments, now reigning over Assyria. The consequent

References and Authorities.

events, as they affected the kingdom of Judah, giving occasion to the most exalted and impassioned prophecies of Isaiah, must be noted in a subsequent section: the immediate result upon the confederacy was most disastrous. First Rezin was overcome and slain, his city of Damascus passed into the hands of the Assyrians, and the Syrian monarchy merged in that of its proud conqueror. Then, by a series of aggressions, chiefly on the northern and eastern parts of the Israelite kingdom, its power was effectually broken. Tiglath-pileser now adopted the new policy of carrying away captives instead of the mere exaction of tribute. Several places are mentioned as captured by him,

1 Kings xv. 20.

named, no doubt, in the succession of his inroads, as no geographical order is observed. First Ijon and Abel-beth-maachah, in the far north, fell a prey to the Assyrian hordes, as they had fallen before to the Syrians under Benhadad. In a yet bolder incursion

Josh. xvi. 6.

the invaders stormed Janoah, a town in the interior, on the border between Ephraim and Manasseh.

Josh. xix. 37.

Kedesh in Naphtali, on the western shore of Lake Merom, and formerly a Levitical city, would fall an easy prey. Hazor, also in Naphtali, an important

2 Kings xiv. 25.

military position, fortified by Solomon, was next subdued. The land of Gilead, east of Jordan, once the prey of Syria, afterwards recovered by Jeroboam II., was then overrun. Galilee, or the "circuit," the border land between Israel and the Gentiles—a smaller territory than that so named in the New Testament—passed into the hands of the Assyrians;

Deut. xxxiv. 23.

and lastly, the remaining portion of the fair land of

Naphtali, once "satisfied with favour and full with the blessing of the Lord," was ravaged and depopulated by the heathen hosts. Such was the first captivity, or rather series of captivities, which too surely heralded the final catastrophe. *References and Authorities.*

§ 2.—Hoshea and the End of the Monarchy.

The reign of Pekah, like that of so many of his predecessors, was brought to a close by the hand of an assassin. HOSHEA, the son of Elah, inflicted the blow, and for nine years more occupied the vassal throne of Israel, until at length the power of Assyria swooped down upon the land and brought the kingdom to an end. Personally, Hoshea seems to have been better disposed than many of the preceding kings. "He did that which was evil in the sight of the Lord, but not as the kings of Israel that were before him." His good points, however, whatever they may have been, could not save his kingdom or himself. Shalmaneser was now king of Assyria, and had already extended the Syrian conquests of his predecessor to Tyre and Sidon; descending then southward on both the eastern and western sides, so as to secure at once the coast of the Mediterranean and the territories east of Jordan. Hoshea vainly sought to stem the course of aggression by annual tribute to the Assyrian king; but at last, in his hopelessness, intermitted the gift, endeavouring at the same time to win over So, or Seva (Shebek), king of Egypt, to his cause. This intrigue was soon discovered by Shalmaneser, who seized and imprisoned Hoshea; then, descending in force upon

Hoshea Saviour!
So Deut. xxxii. 44, &c.

Character of Hoshea.

Shalmaneser's conquests.

the Israelite territory, laid siege to Samaria. The prophet Hosea had already predicted the doom of the Israelitish capital; and after bravely standing a siege of three years, the prophecy was too surely fulfilled. Shalmaneser himself had in the meantime died, and the Assyrian kingdom had been grasped by his son Sargon, who appears in the Assyrian monuments as the captor of Samaria. Thus was Ephraim made "desolate in the day of rebuke." "Thy calf, O Samaria, hath cast thee off." Israel had "plowed wickedness," and had reaped iniquity; its "fortresses were spoiled, as Shalman [Shalmaneser] spoiled Beth-arbel [a place inconsiderable in comparison with Samaria] in the day of battle." Tender appeals and warnings from the lips of the same prophet, and of many a messenger of God beside, had been addressed to "Ephraim" without effect; for the time, all is lost: but even Hosea, in his concluding words, kindles into a strain of hope and exultation:—

References and Authorities.

Hos. v. 9; viii. 5; x. 13, 14.

Hos. xiv. 5—8.

"I will be as the dew unto Israel;
He shall grow as the lily
And cast forth his roots as Lebanon.
His branches shall spread,
And his beauty shall be as the olive tree,
And his scent as Lebanon.
They that dwell under his shadow shall return;
They shall revive as the corn, and grow as the vine;
The scent thereof shall be as the wine of Lebanon.
Ephraim shall say,
What have I to do any more with idols?"

Idol-worship had been the national sin; and the Assyrian was but the "rod of God's anger" to chastise the idolatries inseparably connected for ever with the names of Jeroboam, Ahab, and Jezebel, and so deeply ingrained into the habits of the people as to be removed by nothing short of long captivity and dispersion.

References and Authorities.

Samaria having fallen, the whole land was occupied by the Assyrians, who carried the people away, apparently in successive companies, into bondage. Not only was the kingdom of Israel at an end, but the nation itself had virtually disappeared. The ten tribes have no more place in history. From that exile there was no national return, as afterwards there was the return of Judah from beside the waters of Babylon.

See Note D.

The scattered members of this community, with whom we meet at a far later day, had become incorporated with the Jewish nation; either dwelling in Judea or partakers of their dispersion into many lands. Thus Anna the prophetess was of the tribe of Asher. "Twelve tribes scattered abroad" are recognised by the apostle James. And John in Patmos saw the vision of twelve thousand from every tribe sealed with the seal of God and ransomed by the blood of the Lamb. For us, in Him with whom is "neither Jew nor Gentile," the true "commonwealth of Israel" is the CHURCH OF CHRIST.

Luke ii. 36.
James i. 1.

Rev. vii. 5—8. Here Ephraim is termed *Joseph*, and Dan is missing.

A very striking notice of the mixed nation that succeeded the heritage of Israel closes this section of the inspired history. One of the first measures of the Assyrian monarch was to place bands of colonists in the depopulated territory. The work of colonization was evidently gradual, as we learn from an incidental

References and Authorities.
Ezra iv. 2.

notice in Ezra that some of the settlers were placed in the country by Esarhaddon, son of Sennacherib and grandson of Sargon. These colonists were idolaters, and were soon disturbed in the possession of the land which they had made their own. "They feared not

Therefore in
E.V. 1 Kings
xvii. 25. Heb
simply *and*.

Jehovah; and Jehovah sent lions among them, which slew some of them." The lion, which in ancient times had been often seen in the rocky valleys of Palestine, but which had been driven back by the growth of population, though still prowling among the deep Jordan ravines, now came up boldly into the thinly peopled territory, and stirred the superstitious alarms of the inhabitants. Imagining "the God of the land" to be a local deity, they sent to the king of Assyria to inquire how best to meet his wrath. That monarch commissioned one of the captive priests to instruct the heathen community, not indeed to serve Jehovah only, but to add His name to that of the other gods whom they reverenced. The priest could hardly have been one of the descendants of Aaron, or of the Levitical line. The place where he fixed his

Bethel.

abode, as well as the nature of the transaction, suggests that he was one of the calf-priests established by Jeroboam at Dan and Bethel, and selected as we

See page 19.

know from the tribes indiscriminately. The teaching of such a man would do little to wean the Assyrian settlers from their idolatry. Rather would the worship of Jehovah himself become a kind of heathenism. Some common ground was discovered on which the Israelite remnant could join in worship with the immigrants from Assyria. In modern phrase, they met on "the basis of a common toleration," the Israelites forgetting that the God of their fathers declared Himself to be God alone! So Jehovah was for the time held in honour together with "Nergal and Ashima and Nibhaz and Tartak." The sacrifices on the "high places" still sent up their smoke to heaven, while "the Sepharvites burnt their children in fire to Adrammelech and Anammelech." Never was there a stronger attempt to combine the true and the false in one system of mutual harmony! "The people feared the Lord, and served their own gods."

References and Authorities.

Out of this motley religion arose the SAMARITAN community, so conspicuous in after time. No doubt the national elements became at length commingled. The families of Israelites which remained scattered through the land would intermarry with those of the settlers. By degrees the Assyrian idols lost their hold upon the people, who became nominally the worshippers of the God of Israel. The history of the rancorous opposition offered by the Samaritans to the Jews after the return of the latter from captivity— the erection of the rival temple upon Mount Gerizim, and the bitter strife ensuing—belongs to later periods. To every Christian the Samaritan name is happily and inseparably associated with the declaration made at the foot of Mount Gerizim by One who had come to unveil to all men the secret of the Father's love: "The hour cometh, and now is, when ye shall neither in this mountain, nor yet at Jerusalem, worship the Father. God is a Spirit: and they that worship Him must worship Him in spirit and in truth."

The Samaritans.

John iv. 21, 24.

§ 3.—UZZIAH.

Asa and Uzziah compared.

The observation already made in reference to Asa, that he exercised a long and peaceful reign while Israel was passing through troubled times, under the rule of successive kings, may be almost repeated of UZZIAH. This sovereign was already king in Jerusalem when Jeroboam II. died, and the prosperity of Israel suffered its last eclipse. Uzziah witnessed the brief rule of Zachariah and the yet briefer course of Shallum the murderer and usurper. The cruel Menahem, and Pekahiah his son, were successively Uzziah's contemporaries; and it was not until the Israelite dynasty had again been changed by assassination, and Pekah was upon the throne, that the great Judæan monarch passed away. His full name was

Gesenius, Lex.

AZARIAH: it is by the popular abbreviation "Uzziah" that he is generally known. He occupied the throne longer than any other prince of the house of David,

Fifty-two years.

and though a melancholy calamity marked the close of his reign, it was upon the whole not only prosperous, but splendid. Isaiah was his biographer, and although the full history of the king's life is lost, it was most probably from the prophet's own memoir that the

2 Chron. xxvi.

inspired chronicler compiled the deeply interesting record that survives.

Popular choice and enthusiasm.

The first point noted in Uzziah's reign is that "all the people of Judah" took him, though but a youth of sixteen, and "made him king." Amaziah had fallen by assassin hands; but if the conspirators imagined that they could thus alienate the inheritance of David, they were at once undeceived. The attachment of the people to the royal line, and, may we not add? their appreciation of the divine purpose, were too deep to be shaken by the errors or by the fate of any one king. If loyalty to Amaziah wavered, sorely tried as it must have been by that monarch's mistakes, it rallied on his death in full strength around his son, and Uzziah began his long eventful reign amid an outburst of popular enthusiasm, justified on the whole by his career.

References and Authorities.

His first recorded act is thus simply narrated:— "He built Elath or Eloth, and restored it to Judah." This measure was one of signal policy. Elath was a port of the Red Sea at the head of the Gulf of Akabah, near Ezion-geber. It had been held by Solomon as a naval station, but was lost by Judah in the revolt of the Edomites in the days of Jehoram. Uzziah now reclaimed it, no doubt with a view to commercial enterprise, and his possession of the port no doubt accounts for much of his commercial prosperity.

Elath, on the Red Sea.

1 Kings ix. 26.

In military enterprise his success was decisive. The Philistines, who had been held by Jehoshaphat under tribute, but had rebelled in the days of Jehoram, were again brought into subjection. Gath, that had been seized by Hazael and the Syrians, but had probably reverted to the Philistines, was taken by Uzziah, its fortifications being destroyed, while a yet more important advantage was secured in the capture of the hitherto unconquered Ashdod, a fortress com-

Uzziah's wars.
2 Chron. xvii. 11. xxi. 16.

2 Kings xii. 17.

K

manding the main route to Egypt. Surrounding nations, witnessing the prowess of the Judæan king, became tributary to him; and having obtained a hold upon the wandering tribes of the southern wilderness on both sides of the Dead Sea, he was enabled to provide for the pasture of innumerable flocks and herds. "Three pasture districts are mentioned: one, the 'wilderness,' or high tract to the south and south-east, extending from the western shores of the Dead Sea to the vicinity of Beersheba; (2) the 'low country,' or maritime plain on the west, between the hills of Judea and the sea; and (3) the 'downs,' or rich grazing land beyond the Jordan, on the plateau of Gilead. Uzziah's possession of this last-named district must have been connected with the submission of the Ammonites."

The efficient fortification of Jerusalem, and the enrolment of a strong standing army, also engaged the king's attention. The numbers of the army are specified with exactness, as from some contemporary official record. In the days of Amaziah the number had been 300,000; now there are 307,500, officered by 2,600 chiefs. The insight given into the methods of ancient warfare, by the enumeration of the weapons provided, with the military engines "to cast arrows," like the Roman *catapult*, and "great stones," like the *balista*, is vivid and interesting. These engines, it is suggested with great probability, were invented in Assyria, and thence transferred to Palestine.

Thus far the delineation is that of a powerful monarch, prosperous in commerce, rich in agricultural resources, practised and determined in the arts of war. In the language of inspiration, he was "marvellously helped." God was with him and made him strong. But in the end this strength was his undoing. "His heart was lifted up to his destruction," or "to do wickedly." Let not the crime for which he suffered be esteemed a trivial offence. If one thing was clear in the ordinances which God gave to Israel, it was the separation of the spiritual function from the temporal rule. Melchisedek, the priestly king of Salem, is a solitary type. In after days the Levitical order was appointed to minister before God, the house of David to rule over God's people. "The order of Melchisedek" waited for One to fulfil it, Himself the great, the only Antitype. Uzziah in his pride laid claim to that prerogative: as though no higher dignity remained to one who had grown so great, he aspired to the place of God's Messiah, the anointed priest and king. In vain the priest, who bore the same name with himself, uttered an indignant protest. The occasion was evidently a great one. A large body of priests was ministering in the sanctuary. Before all the people the sanctity of Jehovah's law was put to the proof, and it was shown that no earthly potentate might disobey. In the very act of sacrilege "the leprosy rose up in the king's forehead" with awful suddenness, and he fled from the courts of the Lord's house stricken, terrified, disgraced, to end his days in solitude and misery. Jewish tradition adds that "the earthquake," noted as a signal event of king Uzziah's days, occurred at this crisis, adding to the

References and Authorities.

Gen. xiv. 18.

Psa. cx. 4.
Heb. vi. 20.

"Azariah the chief priest."

Compare 2 Kings v. : 7.
Lev. xiii. 46.

Amos i. 1.

References and Authorities. portent and terror of the scene. It seems most probable, however, that the event happened towards the close of Uzziah's reign, the earthquake having occurred considerably earlier. Jotham, his son, was appointed regent; and when the weary days of the once powerful monarch had ended, the leprosy which had separated him in life from his fellow-men required, according to Hebrew usage, a sepulchre apart from his buried predecessors. That lonely grave in the royal necropolis would eloquently testify to coming generations that all earthly monarchy must bow before the inviolable order of the divine will, and that no interference could be tolerated with that unfolding of the purposes of God which in the fulness of time would reveal the Christ, the true High Priest and King for evermore.

§ 4.—JOTHAM AND AHAZ.

Character of Jotham. Very little is recorded of JOTHAM, the son of Uzziah, excepting, in general terms, that he followed in the footsteps of his father, save in that impious act which had clouded the evening of his reign. Jotham's mother was daughter of Zadok, probably of the priesthood; and the Levitical influence was apparent throughout his reign. One of his most notable works was the erection of a lofty gate to the temple court. He built also upon "the Ophel," the "long, narrowish, rounded spur or promontory which intervenes between the central valley of Jerusalem (the Tyropœon) and the *Geo. Grove.* Kidron, or Valley of Jehoshaphat;" and, at the same time, erected many fortifications in the country districts. With the Ammonites, who appear to have thrown off the yoke imposed upon them by Uzziah, Jotham waged successful war, an additional tribute, distinctly specified, being laid upon them for the three years following the revolt. The only source of real apprehension arose from the designs of Syria, with which power the king of Israel had already entered into alliance, although the full development of their hostile purpose was reserved until the succeeding reign. *[References and Authorities. Revolt of Ammon crushed. 100 talents of silver. 10,000 measures wheat. 10,000 measures barley. Designs of Syria.]*

The melancholy part of the history is conveyed by the inspired writer in the suggestive words, "*The people did yet corruptly.*" How deep and wide-spread was the corruption we may learn from the prophet Isaiah, summoned, as he was, to his high calling in "the year that king Uzziah died." In the first five chapters of his prophecy we have the picture of the nation as it was in the sight of God, most faithfully drawn, and yet most sadly. Punctilious in the routine of ritualistic observances, careful to multiply oblations at the altar, rigorous in the celebration of "new moons and sabbaths, with the calling of assemblies," they had forgotten the primal obligations of justice and charity. Oppression, avarice, and pride everywhere prevailed. Jerusalem itself is laden with the guilt of Sodom, and merits the fate of Gomorrah. Luxury has become the curse of the people. The very daughters of Zion have forgotten their womanly modesty, and flaunt their sumptuous attire in haughty self-display. "Jerusalem is ruined, and Judah is fallen." Already the tokens of divine wrath are at hand. "His anger is *[National corruption. Isa. vi. 1. See Isa. i. 11—17, 21; ii. 8, 9, 11. iii. 9—12, &c. Isa iii. 18-23.]*

not turned away, but His hand is stretched out still." But one way of deliverance is open. Let Judah but repent, and God will be gracious. "Cease to do evil; learn to do well." Thus does Jehovah "reason" with His rebellious people, and in the midst of denunciations and dark forebodings there intervenes a gleam of brightest hope—"the Lord's house established upon the mountains," and "the house of Jacob walking in the light of the Lord."

Isa. ii. 2, 5.

Jotham was young when he inherited the kingdom, and still young when he died. He left the memory of a well-meaning prince, faithful in God's service personally, but without much influence in restraining others. His people, as we have seen, were sunk in ungodliness, and his son and successor, AHAZ, renewed in his own conduct the worst transgressions of former kings. Not only did he sacrifice to Baal and Ashtoreth, but he introduced into Palestine the horrible practice of child-sacrifice to Moloch. For so only can we understand the statement in Kings, "He made his son to pass through the fire," explained as it is by the Chronicler in the words, "He burnt his children in the fire," as though the king gave more than his "firstborn for the sin of his soul." Unhappily, the practice thus introduced by royalty became frequent in after days. Manasseh, grandson of Ahaz, repeated it; and there is no crime of heathenism against which the later prophets more indignantly protest.

On what occasion king Ahaz performed this dreadful sacrifice, we cannot tell. Most probably it was in connection with the earlier troubles that menaced his kingdom, especially from the alliance of Syria and Israel. Two great defeats were suffered by the army of Judah, the confederate powers, as it would seem, attacking them separately. The Syrian forces led a great band of captives triumphantly into Damascus; the restoration of the prisoners taken by the Israelite army has already been narrated. *References and Authorities. Attack by Syria and Israel. See p 121.*

A disaster even more serious than either of these defeats was the loss of Elath, the commercial emporium which Uzziah had regained. The maritime traffic with Arabia, Persia, and the eastern coast of Africa was thus annihilated, and one source of national wealth finally dried up. Dr. Lightfoot remarks that this was the last victory of Syria before it fell under the Assyrian power. *Elath lost.*

Nor did the Judæan kingdom suffer only from these confederate foes. The Edomites, emboldened by the weakness of the monarchy, made inroads from the south-east, carrying off booty and captives, while the Philistines harassed the country from the west, regaining many of their old possessions. On all sides Judah was surrounded by enemies, and it was at this crisis, in the exercise of a sublime faith, as well as in the power of a divine inspiration, that the prophet Isaiah bade the despairing king Ahaz to renounce all human dependence, and trust only in the Lord. But the monarch's faith was not equal to the task, and he took the fatal step of sending to Tiglath-pileser, king of Assyria, for aid against the foes before whom Judah seemed ready to fall. The Assyrian king, exacting a costly tribute as the price *Aggressions of Edom. Isa. vii.*

of his intervention, and no doubt rejoicing in the opportunity of adding Syria and Palestine to his dominions, marched his forces towards Damascus. The two armies met in decisive battle, Syria was utterly defeated, its army dispersed in hopeless rout, while Rezin fled "like a deer" to Damascus for safety. Tiglath-pileser pursued him thither, after crucifying the Syrian generals who had fallen into his hands, and closely invested the capital, destroying the neighbouring towns, laying waste the country, and shutting up Rezin in the city "like a caged bird." Damascus long held out, and Tiglath-pileser, leaving a force sufficient to continue the siege, ravaged, as we have seen, the northern territory of Israel and the country east of the Jordan, only Samaria holding out. The Ammonites, Moabites, Philistines, Edomites, and several Arab tribes successively yielded to the terrible conqueror, the blockade of Damascus meanwhile continuing. At last the city was taken, and Tiglath-pileser, entering in triumph, slew king Rezin and carried many of the inhabitants into captivity. Having thus concluded the war, the Assyrian monarch held a great court in Damascus, to which he summoned the now vassal kings, Ahaz of Judah among the rest. The act of submission was deeply humiliating, nor did Ahaz gain the material advantages for which he had hoped; Tiglath-pileser was apparently master of the situation, and the conquests which had brought deliverance to Judah from the Syrian power had placed her for the time at the mercy of a far more terrible foe.

One occurrence is specially noted in connection with this visit of Ahaz to Damascus. Tiglath-pileser, according to the practice of Assyrian monarchs, had brought an altar thither, which he set up in the conquered city, and on which the tributary kings were required to offer sacrifice. Not only did Ahaz comply with this heathen observance, but he sent the pattern of the altar to Jerusalem to Urijah, the high priest, with directions to make a corresponding one for the temple. The priest obsequiously complied; Solomon's brazen altar was removed from its position in front of the entrance to the holy place, giving to the new altar this place of honour, and setting the former on the north side of the court. The customary sacrifices were for a time offered on this new altar, Ahaz saying, as we should read the words, "As for the brazen altar, it will be for me to inquire [or consider] what I shall do with it." The question, however, was soon settled; Ahaz, with a yet more daring impiety, closed the temple altogether, broke up its sacred vessels, altered or removed part of its costly furniture, and marked his full adoption of polytheistic worship by setting up altars "in every corner of Jerusalem," as well as throughout the land. The Jews still commemorate by a yearly fast this time of affliction.

References and Authorities. "The altar" (Heb.) 2 Kings xvi. 10.

Smith's *Dict. Bible*, vol. ii., p. 54.

2 Chron. iv. 1. Urijah seems to have at first placed the new altar in front of the old.

2 Kings xvi. 15. See *Spk. Comm.*

2 Kings xvi. 18. "The covert" was probably a canopied chair of state for the king during the Sabbath service.

But the designs of the impious king were brought to a sudden close by his death, which occurred in the sixteenth of his reign. The lesson of his career is embodied in a single sentence, "*In the time of his distress did he trespass yet more against the Lord.*" To all time his history teaches that trial and sorrow

Death of Ahaz.

On his age, see Note.

harden the character, if unsanctified. The "uses of adversity" may truly be sweet, but they may be bitter too, and if so there is no bitterness like theirs.

References and Authorities.

King Ahaz slept with his fathers, and received burial in Jerusalem, but not in the royal sepulchre; the priests and people marking, by this exclusion, their sense of his unworthiness. In the year of his death the prophet Isaiah delivered a remarkable prophecy against the Philistines, who had been emboldened throughout this reign in their aggressions against Judah by the weakness of the king, in comparison with the prowess of Uzziah. "Palestina," or Philistia, would now again be smitten down, not only by the successor of Ahaz, but by the dread power of "the north," that is, of Assyria. But while, like a cloud of "smoke," the desolation should come down upon their land, Judah should be secure, and to "the messengers of the nation" sent to inquire, to intimidate, or to threaten, the answer would be given, *that the Lord had founded Zion, and the poor of the people shall trust in it.* All this was abundantly fulfilled in the prosperous reign of HEZEKIAH.

Burial of Ahaz. Comp. 2 Chron xxi. 20; xxiv. 25; xxvi. 23.

Isaiah xiv. 28—32.

§ 5.—HEZEKIAH, KING OF JUDAH.

When the son of Ahaz ascended the throne at the age of twenty-five, his earliest concern was to re-open the sanctuary, "in the first year of his reign, in the first month," as it is emphatically recorded. At other times the priests and Levites were the readiest to act, and kings were led by their advice; in this instance the king was foremost, summoning the ecclesiastical

Accession of Hezekiah.

Nisan, first month of the year: perhaps, also, first of the reign.

functionaries of Judah to a great assembly in an open space before the eastern gate of the temple, and addressing them in an exhortation of much tenderness and power. "Our fathers," he says, "have trespassed." It has been well remarked, "He saith not, *my father*, because it became him, as a son, to be as tender as might be of his father's name, and because his father would not have done all this if their fathers had not neglected their duty." Urijah the priest had joined with Ahaz in setting up an idolatrous altar. The king's word stimulated all to exertion; in eight days the courts were purified, the brazen altar was reinstated, and the sacred vessels were restored; in eight days more the temple was cleansed to its inmost shrine. Then a great sin offering was presented on behalf of the people—"for *all Israel*," as the Chronicler emphatically states, the nation being still ideally one, and the ten tribes, though on the eve of ruin and dispersion, being recognised as the heritage of Jehovah. Provision was made, in connection with this solemn sacrifice, for the reorganization of the temple choir.

References and Authorities.

Matthew Henry.

"And when the burnt offering began, the song of the Lord began also with the trumpets, and with the instruments ordained by David, king of Israel. And all the congregation worshipped, and the singers sang, and the trumpeters sounded, and all this continued until the burnt offering was finished. And when they had made an end of offering, the king and all that were present with him bowed themselves and worshipped."

References and Authorities.

The "burnt offering," the "thank offering," and the "peace offering" severally followed, presented with royal profusion as well as with the excitement of a hallowed joy. Perhaps there is no part of the history which more clearly illustrates the distinction between the various classes of sacrifice. First, the sin offering typified *expiation;* the putting away of sin, without which there could be no reconciliation to God; then the "burnt offering" denoted *consecration*, the individual or the nation presenting it symbolizing, by the total consumption of the victim in the sacrificial flame, the entireness of self-dedication to God; the "thank offering" told of *gratitude*, and the "peace offering" of *communion* with God, the chief emblem in the latter being the sacrificial feast, in which the priests and worshippers united in the temple courts. With free and joyful hearts their offerings were all now presented; the inferior servants of the temple showed even more ready alacrity than the priests; and the king and people gave thanks together for the great and sudden reformation. Even while the national faith and worship had seemed lost, there were secret impulses, hopes, and prayers throughout the land. "God had prepared the people," and the suddenness of the change at last did but evince the power of His hidden, long-continued, mighty working in the hearts of the devout.

The great Passover.

Emboldened by these "tokens for good," the young king took measures for holding a passover, on an almost unexampled scale of magnificence and solemnity. Although too late for the celebration of the festival at the appointed time, the king, with the advice of his counsellors and people, resolved upon its immediate observance. It was a case in which the spirit of worship was superior to the form, and stands in strongest contrast with the will-worship of Jeroboam. Both kings postponed a festival; but in the one case it was arrogant impiety, in the other true and acceptable service. Long details are given by the inspired chronicler of this memorable celebration. Perhaps the most noteworthy fact in connection with it is the cordial invitation which was sent by Hezekiah to the tribes of the northern kingdom to unite with Judah in the festival. The letter, dictated no doubt by Hezekiah himself, is a masterpiece of affectionate pleading. Jewish tradition asserts, not improbably, that Shalmaneser, in his first onslaught upon Israel, had carried away the golden calf from Dan, and that the Israelites of the north, being thus deprived of their idol, were better prepared to receive the summons to go up to the house of Jehovah. It is added that king Hoshea, instead of thwarting his subjects, encouraged them to obey the invitation, removing from the frontier of the land of Judah the guards which had been placed there by his predecessors to hinder the tribes from resorting to Jerusalem. Whatever truth there may be in the tradition, the fact is certain, that many of the Israelites "humbled themselves," and came to the great festival. Others repudiated Hezekiah's message, and laughed his messengers to scorn. It was the final appeal of divine longsuffering to the alienated tribes. But two

References and Authorities.

Postponement allowed in individual cases, Num. ix. 10, 11.

References and Authorities. years more, and the Assyrian foe would be before Samaria; three years longer, and the royal house of Israel would fall, and the era of exile would begin.

The spirit above the rite. In all respects the national celebration was worthy of its preliminaries; nor least in the noble anti-ritualistic spirit in which the king met the mistakes and failures which could not but attend a ceremonial so hastily prepared. His prayer for sincere worshippers, who had failed in some part or other of the outward rite, anticipated the liberty of gospel teaching, and teaches a lesson to all time: *The good Lord pardon every one that prepareth his heart to seek God, the Lord God of his fathers, though he be not cleansed according to the purification of the sanctuary.*

Solomon's feast lasted 14 days. 2 Chron. vii 9. "So there was great joy in Jerusalem, for since the time of Solomon, the son of David, king of Israel, there was not the like in Jerusalem. Then the priests the Levites arose and blessed the people; and their voice was heard, and their prayer came up to His holy dwelling place, even unto heaven."

A second David. Hezekiah was in truth a second David; his zeal for the honour of God inspired a like fervour among the people. From that paschal celebration the worshippers went forth not only to Judah and Benjamin, but to Ephraim and Manasseh, bent upon destroying every symbol of the old idolatry. The *The brazen serpent.* king himself set the example; and it is especially recorded that he destroyed one most venerable historical relic, now more than seven hundred *Num. xxi. 9.* years old, the "serpent of brass" that Moses had made in the wilderness—a priceless monument of

God's mercy to His people. But the very sanctity of the memories that attached to it had led the people into a snare. The most precious memorials must be destroyed and cast away rather than they should become idols. Hezekiah found that people burned incense to this brazen serpent. Had Asa or Jehoshaphat in their reforms been aware of this fact, they would no doubt have made away with the relic. Hezekiah did so now, calling it contemptuously *Nehushtan*—a "bit of copper." *References and Authorities. Some interpret: "it was called" —i.e., by the people.*

Nor was the king content with the work of destruction. With his iconoclastic fervour he conjoined wonderful constructive and organizing power. By prompt, energetic measures he re-instituted the priestly order, and so effectually provided for its maintenance, that the contribution was far more than sufficient for the need. The king himself was astonished when he beheld the "great store" which his appeal had elicited from the "liberality of Israel and Judah." *Measures of organization.*

Thus gloriously did this reign begin. Darker shadows were indeed to fall, with sad and strange reverses, which belong to a later section of the history. Before Hezekiah had been four years on the throne of Jerusalem, the Assyrians had captured Samaria, and the captivity of Israel closes the annals of the separated kingdoms. Henceforth Judah and Benjamin, with the immigrants from the ten tribes, constituted the only Israelite kingdom; threatened almost to the end of Hezekiah's reign by the Assyrian power, delivered by sudden miraculous interpositions, and preserved through many vicissitudes for a hundred and thirty *Coming shadows. Fall of Samaria. Menaces from Assyria.*

References and Authorities. years longer before they fell for a time before the greater might of Babylon.

Babylon. End of this section of the history. The History of the Judæan kings and prophets, of the Captivity and the Return, to the close of the Old Testament Canon, will form the second part of the present work.

NOTES TO CHAPTER V.

A.—THE PARALLEL HISTORIES.

I. NARRATIVES COMMON TO KINGS AND CHRONICLES.

Beginning of Uzziah's reign, 2 Kings xv. 1—4; 2 Chron. xxvi. 3, 4. The same account, except that the "high places" are mentioned only in Kings.

End of Uzziah's reign: his leprosy, 2 Kings xv. 5—7; 2 Chron. xxvi. 21—23. This has characteristic additions by the Chronicler.

2 Kings xv. 5—7.

"And the Lord smote the king, so that he was a leper unto the day of his death, and dwelt in a several house. And Jotham the king's son was over the house, judging the people of the land. And the rest of the acts of Azariah, and all that he did, are they not written in the book of the chronicles of the kings of Judah? So Azariah slept with his fathers; and they buried him with his fathers in the city of David: and Jotham his son reigned in his stead."

2 Chron. xxvi. 21—23.

"And Uzziah the king was a leper unto the day of his death, and dwelt in a several house, being a leper; for he was cut off from the house of the Lord: and Jotham his son was over the king's house, judging the people of the land. Now the rest of the acts of Uzziah, first and last, did Isaiah the prophet, the son of Amoz, write. So Uzziah slept with his fathers, and they buried him with his fathers in the field of the burial which belonged to the kings; for they said, He is a leper; and Jotham his son reigned in his stead."

Accession and reign of Jotham, 2 Kings xv. 32—36; 2 Chron. xxvii. 1—3, 7, 8. The same account substantially, with characteristic additions in the two books. Thus *References and Authorities* in the Kings there is again a reference to the "high places," and the Chronicler is careful to state that Jotham "went not," as Uzziah had gone, "into the temple of the Lord."

End of Jotham's reign, 2 Kings xv. 38; 2 Chron. xxvii. 9; the same substantially.

Accession and early days of Ahaz. Assault by Rezin and Pekah. Assyrian help implored by Judah, 2 Kings xvi. 1—9; 2 Chron. xxviii. 1—8, 16—21. The accounts here are independent, and the comparison will be found very interesting.

2 Kings xvi. 1—9 (margin: 2 Kings xvi. 1—9; 2 Chron. xxviii. 1—8; 16—21.)

2 KINGS xvi. 1—9.

"In the seventeenth year of Pekah the son of Remaliah, Ahaz the son of Jotham king of Judah began to reign. Twenty years old was Ahaz when he began to reign, and reigned sixteen years in Jerusalem, and did not that which was right in the sight of the Lord his God, like David his father. But he walked in the way of the kings of Israel, yea, and made his son to pass through the fire, according to the abominations of the heathen, whom the Lord cast out from before the children of Israel. And he sacrificed and burnt incense in the high places, and on the hills, and under every green tree. Then Rezin king of Syria and Pekah son of Remaliah king of Israel came up to Jerusalem to war: and they besieged Ahaz, but could not overcome him. At that time Rezin king of Syria recovered Elath to Syria, and drave the Jews from Elath: and the Syrians came to Elath, and dwelt there unto this day. So Ahaz sent messengers to Tiglath-pileser king of Assyria, saying, I am thy servant and thy son: come up, and save me out of the hand of the king of Syria, and out of the hand of the king of Israel, which rise up against me. And Ahaz took the silver and gold that was found in the house of the Lord, and in the treasures of the king's house, and sent it for a present to the king of Assyria. And the king of Assyria hearkened unto him: for the king of Assyria went up against Damascus, and took it, and carried the people of it captive to Kir, and slew Rezin."

2 CHRONICLES xxviii. 1—8; 16—21.

"Ahaz was twenty years old when he began to reign, and he reigned sixteen years in Jerusalem: but he did not that which was right in the sight of the Lord, like David his father: for he walked in the ways of the kings of Israel, and made also molten images for Baalim. Moreover he burnt incense [or offered sacrifice] in the valley of the son of Hinnom, and burnt his children in the fire, after the abominations of the heathen whom the Lord had cast out before the children of Israel. He sacrificed also and burnt incense in the high places, and on the hills, and under every green tree.

"Wherefore the Lord his God delivered him into the hand of the king of Syria; and they smote him, and carried away a great multitude of them captives, and brought them to Damascus. And he was also delivered into the hand of the king of Israel, who smote him with a great slaughter. For Pekah the son of Remaliah slew in Judah an hundred and twenty thousand in one day, which were all valiant men; because they had forsaken the Lord God of their fathers. And Zichri, a mighty man of Ephraim, slew Maaseiah the king's son, and Azrikam the governor of the house, and Elkanah that was next to the king. And the children of Israel carried away captive of their brethren two hundred thousand, women, sons, and daughters, and took also away much spoil from them, and brought the spoil to Samaria.

"At that time did king Ahaz send unto the kings of Assyria to help him. For again the Edomites had come and smitten Judah, and carried away captives. The Philistines also had invaded the cities of the low country, and of the south of Judah, and had taken Beth-shemesh, and Ajalon, and Gederoth, and Shocho with the villages thereof, and Timnah with the villages thereof, Gimzo also and the villages thereof: and they dwelt there. For the Lord brought Judah low because of Ahaz king of Israel; for he made Judah naked, and transgressed sore against the Lord. And Tilgath-pilneser king of Assyria came unto him, and distressed him, but strengthened him not. For Ahaz took away a portion out of the house of the Lord, and out of the house of the king, and of the princes, and gave it unto the king of Assyria: but he helped him not."

Idolatry of Ahaz: after his visit to Damascus, 2 Kings xvi. 10—18; 2 Chron. xxviii. 22—25. It is evident that these accounts also are independent. That in the Kings has much more of detail.

2 KINGS xvi. 10—18.

"And king Ahaz went to Damascus to meet Tiglath-pileser king of Assyria, and saw an altar that was at Damascus: and king Ahaz sent to Urijah the priest the fashion of the altar, and the pattern of it, according to all the workmanship thereof. And Urijah the priest built an altar according to all that king Ahaz had sent from Damascus: so Urijah the priest made it against king Ahaz came from Damascus. And when the king was come from Damascus, the king saw the altar: and the king approached to the altar, and offered thereon. And he burnt his burnt offering and his meat offering, and poured his drink offering, and sprinkled the blood of his peace offerings, upon the altar. And he brought also the brasen altar, which was before the Lord, from the forefront of the house, from between the altar and the house of the Lord, and put it on the north side of the altar. And king Ahaz commanded Urijah the priest, saying, Upon the great altar burn the morning burnt offering, and the evening meat offering, and the king's burnt sacrifice, and his meat offering, with the burnt offering of all the people of the land, and their meat offering, and their drink offerings; and sprinkle upon it all the blood of the burnt offering, and all the blood of the sacrifice: and the brasen altar shall be for me to inquire by. Thus did Urijah the priest according to all that king Ahaz commanded. And king Ahaz cut off the borders of the bases, and removed the laver from off them; and took down the sea from off the brasen oxen that were under it, and put it upon a pavement of stones. And the covert for the sabbath that they had built in the house, and the king's entry without, turned he from the house of the Lord for the king of Assyria."

2 CHRONICLES xxviii. 22—25.

"And in the time of his distress did he trespass yet more against the Lord: this is that king Ahaz. For he sacrificed unto the gods of Damascus, which smote him: and he said, Because the gods of the kings of Syria help them, therefore will I sacrifice to them, that they may help me. But they were the ruin of him, and of all Israel. And Ahaz gathered together the vessels of the house of God, and cut in pieces the vessels of the house of God, and shut up the doors of the house of the Lord, and he made him altars in every corner of Jerusalem. And in every several city of Judah he made high places to burn incense unto other gods, and provoked to anger the Lord God of his fathers."

Death of Ahaz, 2 Kings xvi. 19, 20 ; 2 Chron. xxviii. 26, 27 ; the same paragraph, save that the Chronicler adds, "they brought him not into the sepulchres of the kings of Israel."

Accession of Hezekiah, 2 Kings xviii. 1—3 ; 2 Chron. xxix. 1, 2 ; almost identical. The mother's name is given as *Abi* in the former, *Abijah* in the latter.

II. Sections peculiar to the Kings.

Reigns of Shallum and Menahem, 2 Kings xv. 13—22.

Reign of Pekahiah, chap. xv. 23—26.

Reign of Pekah, chap. xv. 27, 28.

Assassination of Pekah by Hoshea, chap. xv. 30, 31.

Reign of Hoshea, invasion by the Assyrians, captivity of Israel, Assyrian Settlements and Samaritan idolatry, chap. xvii., xviii. 9—12 ; this last account a repetition.

Character of Hezekiah: he destroys the graven images and "Nehushtan": his early victories, chap. xviii. 1—8.

III. Sections peculiar to the Chronicles.

Details of Uzziah's reign ; his sacrilege and punishment, 2 Chron. xxvi. 5—21.

Jotham's greatness; he subdues the Ammonites, chap. xxvii. 4—6.

Captives of Judah carried by Pekah to Samaria, and delivered on the interposition of the prophet Oded, chap. xxviii. 8—15.

Religious reforms by Hezekiah : repair and purification of the temple, great passover, reorganization of the Levitical order, chap. xxix. 9—36 ; xxx., xxxi.

IV. Fragments of History in the Book of Isaiah. *References and Authorities.*
The Invasion of Pekah and Rezin; Sign given to Ahaz, Isa. vii. 1—16.
Birth of Isaiah's son : his name is a forewarning of the subjugation of Syria and Israel by the Assyrian power, chap. viii. 1—4.

B.—Assyria and Israel.

The monuments of Assyria, recently discovered, enable us to trace much of its early history, and to note some interesting points of connection with the sacred record.

From Gen. x. we learn that the Assyrians were originally a colony from Babylonia. "Out of that land went forth Asshur" (in a northerly direction, towards the higher part of the Tigris), "and builded Nineveh, and the city Rehoboth, and Calah, and Resen between Nineveh and Calah." "In the inscriptions known to us," writes the late Mr. George Smith, "no account of the origin of 'Syria has yet been discovered; but the religion, literature, method of writing, and science of Assyria are evidently Babylonian in origin, and agree with the statement of Genesis." The date of Asshur is uncertain: the earliest monumental records go back to the nineteenth century B.C., and give a long succession of kings until about 1020 B.C., when the annals of the kingdom sink into obscurity for 150 years. "It is a curious fact," says Mr. Smith, "that this period of decline in the Assyrian power synchronizes with the rise of the Hebrew monarchy. A powerful Syrian empire was founded at Zobah, and David, king of Israel, having defeated Hadar-ezer, king of Zobah, subdued all the kings as far as the river Euphrates. The Jewish power, now under David, and Solomon his son, took the place formerly occupied by the Assyrian monarchs; but on the breaking up of this empire on the death of Solomon, the Jews at once lost their supremacy."

Gen. x. 11, 12.

"Assyria" *(Ancient History from the Monuments,* C.K.S.,p.21.)

Assyria, p. 35.

Soon after the death of Solomon the Assyrian monuments begin again to record a succession of conquests and the extension of the empire.

The following list of kings is taken from Canon Rawlinson:—
No exact dates prior to B.C. 909, when King Asshur-danin-il I. ceased to reign.

Ancient Monarchies, 29, 30.

References and Authorities.

909. Iva-lush.
889. Tiglathi Nin II.
886. Asshur-idanni-pal I. Sardanapalus.
858. Shalmaneser II.
823. Shamas-Iva.
810. Iva-lush II.—his wife Semiramis.
781. Shalmaneser III.
771. Asshur-danin-il II.; and PUL (?), a rival king, on the Euphrates.
753. Asshur-lush.
745. TIGLATH-PILESER II. (ally of Ahaz against Pekah and Rezin).
727. SHALMANESER IV.—besieges Samaria.
721. SARGON—usurper, captor of Samaria.

The names mentioned in Scripture are denoted by capitals. Sargon, father of Sennacherib, is only mentioned once (Isa. xx. 1), but the monuments point to him clearly as the captor of Samaria, and the settlement of the inhabitants (27,280 families, according to his own statement) "in Halah and on the Habor *Canon* (Khabour) the river of Gozan, and (at a later period pro- *Rawl'nson,* bably) in the cities of the Medes." Canon Rawlinson adds, *Smith's Dict. Bible,* "There is a peculiarity of phraseology in 2 Kings xviii. 9, 10, *art. Sargon.* which perhaps indicates a knowledge on the part of the writer that Shalmaneser was not the actual captor. 'In the fourth year of Hezekiah Shalmaneser king of Assyria came up against Samaria, and besieged it: and at the end of three years THEY took it.'" So in xvii. 6 it is simply said, "the king of Assyria took Samaria," without mentioning any name. No doubt Shalmaneser died during the siege.

"Sargon probably reigned nineteen years, B.C. 721—702, when he left the throne to his son, the celebrated Sennacherib."

C.—PROPHETS OF THE ERA.

I. *Israel.*—HOSEA continued his prophetic work from the days of Jeroboam II. to those of Hoshea, the last of the Israelite kings. It may be well here to notice that the name of the prophet and that of the king are precisely the same, Hoshea and Hosea being two modes of spelling one Hebrew word, "He shall save." Joshua bore the same name in his earlier days, the alteration in his case being for the purpose of incorporating with the name the word JEHOVAH—"Jehovah shall save," or, "Salvation of Jehovah." Joshua, again, it is well known, is the same with *Jesus* (Acts vii. 45 ; Heb. iv. 8).

1. *Micah*, of Moresheth-Gath (chap. i. 14 :—a town of Judah near the Philistine frontier, west of Jerusalem), prophesied in the days of Jotham, Ahaz, and Hezekiah, B.C. 757—699. See also Jer. xxvi. 18, which literally quotes Micah iii. 12. He predicts the destruction of Samaria by the Assyrians, chap. i. 6—8 ; and vividly describes the Assyrian invasion of Judah, foretelling its failure ; but pointing onward to the coming Babylonian attack, with the consequent calamities.

But further reference to Micah's prophecies, as well as to those of his greater contemporary *Isaiah*, may more properly be referred to the second division of the present work.

2. *Isaiah*, son of Amoz (not of Amos the prophet, a different word), was called to the prophetic office "in the year that king Uzziah died," about B.C. 758, and continued his ministry for sixty years. It will be requisite hereafter to notice the connection of his prophecies with the history of the times.

D.—THE TEN TRIBES.

"There has been a widespread belief among modern Christians that the ten tribes, having never returned to their native country, must still exist somewhere in a collected body. Travellers have thought to discover them in Malabar, in Kashmir, in China, in Turkistan, in Affghanistan, in the Kurdish mountains, in Arabia, in Germany, in North America. Books have been written advocating this or that identification, and the notion has thus obtained extensive currency that somewhere or other in the world the descendants of the ten tribes must exist, and that when found they might be recognised as such by careful and diligent inquiry. It seems to have been forgotten that, in the first place, they were scattered over a wide extent of country (Harran, Chalcitis, Goyan or Mygdonia, and Media) by the original conqueror ; that, secondly, in the numerous conquests and changes of population which are known to have taken place in these regions, they would naturally become more scattered ; that, thirdly, a considerable number of them probably returned with the Jews under

Zerubbabel and Ezra (Ezra vi. 16; viii. 35; 1 Chron. ix. 3); that, fourthly, those who remained behind would naturally either mingle with the heathen among whom they lived, or become united with the Jews of the dispersion; and that, fifthly, if there had been anywhere in this part of Asia at the time of Alexander's conquests or of the Roman expeditions against Parthia and Persia a community of the peculiar character supposed, it is most improbable that no Greek or Roman historian or geographer should have mentioned it. Against these arguments there is nothing to be set but the statement of Josephus, in the first century of our era, that the ten tribes still existed beyond the Euphrates (he does not say in a collective form) at his day (*Ant.* xi. 5, § 2), and a similar declaration of Jerome in the fifth. Neither writer has any personal acquaintance with the countries, or speaks from his own knowledge. Both may be regarded as relating rather what they supposed must be than what they knew actually was the case. Again, neither may mean more than that among the Hebrews of the dispersion (Acts ii. 9; Philo, "Leg. ad Cai." p. 1031), in Parthia, Media, Elam, and Mesopotamia, were many Israelites. On the whole, therefore, it would seem probable (1) that the ten tribes never formed a community in their exile, but were scattered from the first; and (2) that their descendants either blended with the heathen and were absorbed, or returned to Palestine with Zerubbabel and Ezra, or became inseparably united with the dispersed Jews in Mesopotamia and the adjacent countries. No discovery, therefore, of the ten tribes is to be expected, nor can works written to prove their identity with any existing race or body of persons be regarded as anything more than ingenious exercitations."—Canon Rawlinson, in the *Speaker's Commentary*.

TABLES OF
CONTEMPORARY HISTORY,

254 YEARS. B.C. 975—721.

ISRAEL.

B.C.
975. Jeroboam, son of Nebat.
954. Nadab, son of Jeroboam.

953. Baasha, son of Ahijah of Issachar.
930. Elah, son of Baasha.

929. (Zimri, Tibni), Omri.
918. Ahab, son of Omri.
898. Ahaziah, son of Ahab and Jezebel.
896. Jehoram, son of Ahab and Jezebel.

884. Jehu, son of Nimshi.
856. Jehoahaz, son of Jehu.
840. Jehoash, or Joash, son of Jehoahaz.
825. Jeroboam II., son of Joash.
784. Interregnum.
774. Zachariah, son of Jeroboam II.

773. (Shallum), Menahem.
762. Pekahiah, son of Menahem.

760. Pekah.

730. Hoshea.
721. Fall of Samaria, after a siege begun by Shalmaneser, continued by Sargon.

JUDAH.

B.C.
- 975. Rehoboam, son of Solomon and Naamah, an Ammonitess.
- 958. Abijam, son of Rehoboam and Maachah, descendant of Absalom.
- 955. Asa, son of Abijam (and grandson of Maachah).
- 914. Jehoshaphat, son of Asa and Azubah, daughter of Shilhi.
- 889. Jehoram, son of Jehoshaphat.
- 885. Ahaziah, son of Jehoram and Athaliah.
- 884. Usurpation by Athaliah (daughter of Ahab and Jezebel).
- 878. Joash, son of Ahaziah and Zibiah of Beersheba.
- 839. Amaziah, son of Joash and Jehoaddan of Jerusalem.
- 811. Azariah (Uzziah), son of Amaziah and Jecoliah.
- 759. Jotham, son of Uzziah and Jerusha, daughter of Zadok.
- 743. Ahaz, son of Jotham.
- 727. Hezekiah, son of Ahaz and Abijah, daughter of Zechariah.

Still reigning, B.C. 721.

₊ It will be observed that the *mother's* name is generally given in the case of the kings of Judah ; hardly ever in that of the kings of Israel. Of the two worst of the kings, Jehoram and Ahaz, the mother's name is omitted.

OTHER NATIONS.

B.C.
- Babylonia, subject to Assyria from B.C. 1250.
- Twenty-second Egyptian dynasty, B.C. 993.
- 975. Sheshonk, or Shishak, reigning in Egypt to B.C. 972.
- 956. Osorkon II., king of Egypt (probably Zerah, the invader of Judah).
- 955. Agesilaus in Sparta.
- 944. The poet Hesiod in Greece.
- 900. Homer flourished about this time.
- 898. Lycurgus in Sparta.
- 869. Carthage founded by the Phœnician queen, Dido.
- 847. Twenty-third Egyptian dynasty.
- 820. Empire of the Medes founded by Arbaces.
- 814. Kingdom of Macedon founded by Caranus.

B.C.
776. The computation by Olympiads begins (the Grecian era).
758. Twenty-fourth Egyptian dynasty.
753. Foundation of Rome (A.U.C.—the Roman era).
750. Phrygian monarchy established in Asia Minor.
747. Independence of the Babylonian empire achieved by Nabonassar.
724. Sabaco or Shebek I. (an Ethiopian), king of Egypt, called So in Scripture.
721. First recorded eclipse of the moon, March 19. Merodach-Baladan on the throne of Babylon.

For notices of the Assyrian kings see on the fifth chapter, Note B, p. 149.

www.ingramcontent.com/pod-product-compliance
Lightning Source LLC
Chambersburg PA
CBHW030259170426
43202CB00009B/811